Advance Praise

"Joan's Heart Shift method is a unique blend of spiritual practices and hypnotherapy, creating a powerful way to heal from the inside out. In her book, she shares incredible stories from her clients that highlight this transformative approach. This book not only offers hope and inspiration—it will ignite your passion for your own healing and renewal."

—Mark Anthony Lord,
Spiritual teacher and healer

"Joan Coletto goes deeper and moves you further than most experts because she lives what she teaches. She taps into SOUL. If you want to stop holding yourself back and REALLY live the life you've dreamed of—read this book!"

—Sara Connell,
Bestselling author of *The Science of Getting Rich for Women*

In the words of Joan's Clients:

"From our very first session, I realized not all practitioners are created equal—Joan went straight to the heart of the matter in a way I'd never experienced. She has an uncanny ability to cut through the noise while making me feel completely seen and safe."

"Joan doesn't just nod and hand out generic affirmations; she gives you practical steps and real, honest feedback that challenges you to grow and helps you discover the truth."

Printed in the United States of America

Hardcover ISBN: 978-1-967703-22-7

Paperback ISBN: 978-1-960876-91-1

eBook ISBN: 978-1-967703-23-4

Library of Congress Control Number: 2025944769

Muse Literary Publishing Send feedback to hello@museliterary.com Special discounts for bulk sales are available, please contact operations@museliterary.com

HEART SHIFT

Transform Painful Patterns to Live an Empowered Life

By: Joan Coletto

Contents

*"The soul always knows what to do to heal itself.
The challenge is to silence the mind."*

—Caroline Myss

This book is dedicated to you and your beautiful journey. As you turn these pages, it's my heartfelt wish that the practices and insights within offer you a beacon of hope. May the stories of transformation I have shared strengthen and inspire you to transcend the challenges you may be facing. My greatest hope is that you are moved toward realizing your dreams and encouraged to envision and create a life that resonates with the deepest desires of your heart.

A Note to the Reader

I was the fixer and peacemaker in my family. I was so focused on trying to maintain peace that not only did I not have my emotional needs met, but I didn't even know what those needs were. My compassion for my sibling, who was the target of much of my father's anger, left me feeling guilty that I was never the target.

His anger triggered me so deeply that I was unable to allow myself to be angry. I was terrified of anger. My feelings were so buried that I was unaware of them.

My path to healing was layered, beginning with a traditional therapist, then a spiritual practitioner, and finally hypnotherapy. Every step of the way, I grew and learned beneficial tools and techniques. I use many of these in my work with clients and will be sharing them with you. Each step forward we take prepares us for the next.

My therapist supported me in gaining the courage and confidence to end my first marriage. I came to realize my husband was much like my father—explosive anger, unpredictable behavior, and wide mood swings. Having married him at the age of 20, I had never lived on my own or supported myself. I thought I needed someone to take care of me and felt incapable of supporting myself. I didn't know who I was without him. I had lost touch with old friends and only socialized with "our" friends. He made significantly more money than I did. How would I financially support myself?

I came to understand that I was more than capable of supporting myself and did just that. I knew I was worthy of a loving, mutually supportive relationship and would not settle for less.

Ultimately, my time living alone and supporting myself was one of my greatest learning experiences. I learned that not only was it possible to survive—I learned to thrive.

I began studying spirituality and reading everything I could get my hands on about oneness and the law of attraction. It was several years later, while in my new marriage, that I became active in a spiritual center, which further expanded my consciousness and beliefs. Being part of a community with like-minded individuals supported and strengthened my new belief that I could create the life I desired. Spiritual practices became an integral part of my life. Daily meditation, visualization, and affirmation were diligently maintained. This is also when I began my studies to become a spiritual practitioner.

When I started exploring hypnotherapy as a means to further support my clients, I didn't know the impact it would have on me personally I learned how to express and release anger in a healthy way. I also came to understand that in stuffing down the anger, I didn't allow other emotions to be fully expressed. In practice sessions with colleagues, I uncovered deep-seated beliefs that were impacting my behaviors. I will never forget the day I realized why I was so overprotective of my daughter. From the moment I found out I was pregnant, I was afraid I would lose her. I had several miscarriages prior to her birth, so this made sense. However, I never realized that was the source of my current worry about her. I transitioned from a perpetual state of anxiety to an unprecedented sensation of lightness and ease within my being.

Supporting my clients in living a life they love is an honor and has never felt like work. Training in the world of spirituality taught me many useful techniques, like meditation, visioning, and affirmation. My training in hypnotherapy allowed me to take my clients even deeper into their subconscious and quickly access the root and source of their pain.

I have combined these two modalities and other training in my own unique way and created what I call Heart Shift—a unique fusion of hypnotherapy and spiritual practices.

No matter how dire your circumstances, I fully believe a Heart Shift is possible. Like for Evan, whose journey was transformative. He didn't just manage his physical pain—he was able to completely alleviate it by identifying and releasing the stress that caused it. This empowered him to face whatever challenges came his way. And Maggie, who went from devastation after being betrayed by her boyfriend and friend to freedom and prioritizing her needs. She is now in joyous anticipation of having the kind of relationship she deeply desires and is worthy of.

I knew I had to write this book when I realized that my passion for supporting others required a larger platform in order to reach more people. I have been blessed with amazing mentors, teachers, and healers. The shift that has occurred in my life is a gift that I deeply desire to share with you. I have grown from being painfully shy and withdrawn to creating a life of standing up and being seen. I know fully who I am and what I am capable of. I have helped countless people find their passion in life, release old narratives that were running the show, and more. The "me" of my youth never would have imagined being seen and known in this way.

We all have the innate ability to grow and expand. Your growth and expansion matter. They matter not only to you but to all of those around you. As you experience more love and joy in your life, your loved ones, coworkers, and even strangers will feel that positive energy, and it will leave an impact on them.

In this book, I will share stories of hope—some personal and some from the people I have worked with. What they have in common is the healing that is possible when we Heart Shift. To maintain anonymity, I have changed the names and details and occasionally woven together stories from different people to honor their privacy.

How does Heart Shift work?

Consciousness precedes form. Our thoughts, beliefs, and intentions shape our reality. When we shift our beliefs at the level of the subconscious mind, we can change our life experience, thereby shifting the trajectory of our lives. We still need to take action to bring our desires to fruition; however, when our actions become a reflection of our shift in inner consciousness and intentions, we attract our true desires. As we release and let go of those old stories, we're free to earnestly inquire, "Who am I?

How do I want to show up in the world? What do I desire to experience?" Through visualization and other spiritual practices, we begin to draw those desires to us. Opportunities will present themselves, and we will be guided toward inspired action.

Throughout these chapters, I will share the Seven Pillars, which, in addition to hypnotherapy and other modalities, comprise Heart Shift. While some of the practices I use are considered spiritual, they are not religious, and all that is required is an open mind. It is about tuning in to your authentic self and listening to your internal wisdom.

Included with this book is an online portal where you will find several interactive and downloadable worksheets and recordings to support you on your journey.

It is no accident that you picked up this book. There is a voice within that is telling you that you can have more, you can be more, and you are more than your current circumstances. Perhaps that voice is a gentle whisper, barely perceptible while unwinding at the end of a hectic day. Or perhaps it is an incessant, passionate cry from within, striving to break free. Whatever it is, my hope is that you find the courage and the strength to rewrite your story through Heart Shift so that you see what you most desire is possible and that you are not alone.

PART I

Chapter 1
Creating Heart Shift

I AM A HEALER. There, I said it. Even as a teen, I sensed that this was my calling although I didn't understand the reasons behind it or what it might look like. Friends always came to me for advice. I was the trusted listener and helper, even when my life wasn't necessarily going great. I made some poor choices, particularly in my teens and 20s, and yet somehow, I could see for others what I could not always see for myself.

When I say I am a healer, I do not mean that I have any special powers or some kind of magic. What I mean is that I see the truth of the essence of who you are, and I support you in uncovering that truth for yourself so that you are able to rewrite your story and progress in life in a conscious way. All of the answers to your questions are within you. There is a higher self that is connected to your intuition, and that is the true guide for your life. I am merely the way-shower to support you in tuning in and listening to that inner wisdom using Heart Shift, the method I developed through my training in hypnotherapy, spiritual practice, and other modalities.

Most of us have experienced a "gut feeling." Maybe you were interviewing for a new job or starting a new relationship, and something just didn't feel right. You couldn't necessarily put it into words—it was simply a feeling. Learning how to tune in and understand these feelings and intuitive insights guides us in living a more conscious, happy, and productive life. Heart Shift will support you in learning how to trust this inner wisdom.

My journey of discovering how to connect to that inner wisdom began when I was in my early thirties. After years of miscarriages and infertility, I turned to spirituality and my belief in and understanding of a higher power. I was in a sad and desperate place. I grappled with the uncertainty that the dream I held so dearly—the dream of becoming a mother and building a family alongside my husband—was slipping further away despite how hard I reached for it.

The nights were the hardest. I cried myself to sleep more times than I'd like to admit, stifling my sobs to avoid waking my husband. The therapist I had been working with suggested a book called *The Greatest Thing in the World*, which I found at a little bookstore attached to a spiritual center off Michigan Avenue in Chicago. The book is a metaphysical translation of 1 Corinthians 13 in the New Testament of the Christian Bible and is about love. It speaks to the nine ingredients that make up the spectrum of love: patience, kindness, generosity, humility, courtesy, unselfishness, good temper, guilelessness, and sincerity. These ingredients apply to self-love, romantic love, and love in general. Until the therapist suggested it, it hadn't occurred to me that a Bible passage could be relevant in my life.

As I looked around the bookstore, I saw many amazing titles I had never seen before. These books about peace, spirituality, and love were calling to me and sparking something within me. I felt butterflies in my stomach; I had stepped into something big and beautiful. Standing in that bookstore, a smile spread across my face as I remembered lying awake at night as a young child speaking to God, asking, *"What is going to happen to me?" "Will I always feel scared like this?"*

I knew that after praying, I always felt God's presence, and it calmed me. I felt deep inside that life would get better. I wouldn't always be fearful of anger or afraid to speak up. It's interesting because we weren't a religious family, and what I knew of God was more about a judgmental, punishing figure up in the sky somewhere. Although I was technically raised Greek Orthodox, my family rarely went to church or practiced the religion in any definable way. But deep down at the core of my being, I sensed there was something greater than me and my experience—something of and for good.

This bookstore was the gateway to that hope. I knew that any spiritual center with a bookstore like that had to be a great place. It wasn't until a couple of years later that I asked my husband to join me in attending a Sunday morning service. I learned that the center was transdenominational, meaning it embraced all paths and was not affiliated with any particular religion. It fostered unity and inclusivity rather than adhering to the doctrines of a single tradition.

As I was sitting for the first time at the service, there was a guided meditation. We were instructed, *"Focus on your breath. Inhale fully and exhale completely."* Then, *"Feel yourself connected to everyone in the room, in this city, on this planet."* It almost felt like they were speaking a different language. I had never really been taught the concept of oneness and connection in that way. It was certainly not like any church I had ever been to, and I remember thinking, *I love this place, and I hope my husband doesn't think it's weird.* Fortunately, he also loved it. With his support, I embarked on a deep dive into spirituality that I credit with changing my life. I became more hopeful and positive. I gained confidence and a sense within that I could create a life in which I would thrive.

After that first service, I became very involved in the spiritual center. I jumped in—taking classes, volunteering, and being a part of the community. Through those classes, I learned so much about the power of the mind and how our consciousness creates our experience. I had been struggling with infertility and numerous miscarriages and began shifting my belief system from *"God is out there judging and punishing"* to a deep belief that *"God is of and for good always."* I came to honestly believe that God is ever-present and that its energy is in me and in all people. I knew I could lean into that energy and shift my experience of life to one of joy and hope.

After continuing to attend the Spiritual Center for about a year, I finally became pregnant, carried that child to term, and had a second healthy child, all in my late 30s. This is not to say that some kind of magic happens when you meditate and dive into spirituality. While it was a contributing factor, I also had the aid of doctors and science to support my becoming a mother. It takes commitment and effort to shift beliefs, so although it is actually simple, it is not necessarily easy.

Through my meditation practice and study, I learned to listen to the inner guidance and wisdom that showed me where to go for help and what I needed. The solutions to any challenge are always available. Our work is to pay attention and listen. We may not like the answers we receive, but they lead us to what is in our highest and best interest.

"New Thought" is a spiritual movement that originated in the 19th century. It focuses on metaphysical beliefs and the idea that positive thinking can affect personal outcomes, including health, wealth, and personal happiness. Your thoughts have the power to shape your circumstances, for better or worse. While this outlook has helped many people achieve personal growth and success, it can also be a double-edged sword. What we may not realize is that those thoughts and beliefs are often subconscious, and we aren't necessarily aware of them.

One of the traps of New Thought thinking is the idea that we are to blame for everything that occurs in our lives. This is not true. The truth is that life happens for us and we are here to learn and grow. On some level, we have all chosen our path. That doesn't mean I wanted to have several miscarriages or years of infertility—I definitely did not want that. However, because of those experiences, I had to reach deep into my soul and understand on a much deeper level who I am, what I want, and what really matters in my life.

I deeply wanted children and a family. The longing for a child had become a constant companion in my and my husband's lives. Each month, hope would grow, only to wither away with the passing days. The physical toll of the procedures—the ones I had initially welcomed with open arms—now seemed to weigh heavily on me, both physically and emotionally.

"I just… I thought it would be different," I whispered one evening to my husband.

He held me in his arms. "I know… I know."

There was an unspoken understanding between us.

The idea of adoption surfaced. It was a path filled with its own uncertainties, yet it held a promise—a different kind of hope. While those close to us knew what we were going through and empathized, unless you're actually experiencing it, it's hard to fully grasp what a couple goes through.

"We'll get through this," he said with confidence.

And in that moment, I felt it—the strength of our unity, the resilience of our love.

This utter belief that we would have children might not have happened had I not had those experiences. This is not to say it had to be that way; one does not have to go through pain and heartache to grow. We all have our own paths and ways to grow and expand.

One of the biggest pain points in my first marriage was when I desperately tried to get pregnant and couldn't. In hindsight, I am very grateful that I did not get pregnant at that time in my life. I was not ready to be a mother, and my former husband is not who I would want to be the father of my children. When we are in the midst of pain and suffering, acceptance can feel next to impossible.

Alcoholics Anonymous the Big Book states, "Acceptance is the answer to all my problems today." There is no peace until we accept what is…—exactly as it is. Resistance will not change it. By accepting what we cannot change, we have an opportunity to perhaps look at it in a different way. Sometimes, when something doesn't go our way, it ends up being a blessing. For me, not becoming pregnant with my first husband turned out to be just that.

As time went on, it became more challenging to be a part of the spiritual center I had grown to love so much. They had no place for my two small children to play, which made it hard to bring them. I practiced the things that I learned in classes and at services on my own. It wasn't ideal, but it filled in the gap until we found a spiritual center near our new home that had a youth group.

The center was Christian-based, and although we had both been loosely raised Christian, we appreciated the greater diversity of the transdenominational center. We longed for a spiritual community, and, for a while, the Christian-based center was enough.

At a fundraiser for this spiritual center, we ran into someone who had heard about a new spiritual center in the city that was in alignment with the teachings we had grown to appreciate. It did not adhere to any particular religion and celebrated all life, honoring all traditions and faiths.

We began attending Sunday services regularly, and again, my life was changed. I came to understand the meaning and rich traditions around celebrations such as Hanukkah and Kwanzaa. Although they did not yet have a youth group, our children were a little older and would join us during service. The energy was so alive and engaging! They had an amazing band, and the music was electrifying. Everyone was standing and moving with the music as it uplifted and revitalized us!

I was once again taking classes, volunteering, and becoming very active at the center. I started connecting and forming close relationships with more like-minded people, and I began living in a much deeper way than ever before. The principles I was learning—primarily that we are all one and that our thoughts and beliefs create our reality—literally changed the trajectory of my life.

Meditation had once again become a daily practice, and I learned about visioning, a process in which you tap into a higher consciousness to catch a vision of what you want to create and also realize what you may have to let go of. Visioning became an essential component in creating my private practice. I also began to more fully understand the concept of oneness and came to realize how my actions, thoughts, and beliefs impact others.

The concept that we are all one can in fact transform the way we show up in life. The sense of interconnectedness and release of separation allow us to be more compassionate and empathetic toward our fellow human beings.

Being conscious of our thoughts and choosing positive ones can shift our experience. Imagine your thoughts and beliefs as seeds. These seeds are planted in soil, which represents the environment that nurtures their growth. The resulting plant symbolizes the outcomes you experience in life. In essence, the type of thought or belief you "plant" will be cultivated by the environment, leading to a corresponding experience or outcome. Many of our beliefs are subconscious, and we are not fully aware of them. This is where Heart Shift can support a change in belief and alter the outcome.

As I was taking classes at the new spiritual center, I learned that there was a path to becoming a counselor and coaching individuals. This stirred in me the desire I had always had—to be a guide for others and support them in finding the fulfillment I had found. After two years of taking prerequisite classes and another two years of taking master's-level classes, I became a spiritual practitioner. This enabled me to work with people and be the support I always imagined I would be.

A spiritual practitioner is one who knows the truth of your being: you are whole, perfect, and complete, regardless of what outer circumstances may look like. As a spiritual practitioner, I learned how to use spiritual practices such as meditation, visualization, and affirmation to support the shift in consciousness needed to create positive change. While supporting people in changing painful patterns, I came to realize that it wasn't so much about what happened in someone's life as it was about the story they associated with it.

For example, let's say your parents separated when you were young, and one parent moved out of the house. This naturally created a shift in dynamics, and the way you spent time with them together became different. Holidays looked different. Vacations felt different. As a child, you may have made up a story in your mind that it was somehow your fault—that you weren't good enough or worthy. You may have carried the belief that you caused the change in your life, even though it wasn't true.

Children naturally see themselves as the center of everything, so these thoughts and beliefs are very common. Once you grow into an adult, there is an intellectual understanding that, of course, you didn't cause the divorce. It was something that happened between two adults, and these things happen. However, deep down within you, the child who lived through the divorce still wants to blame you for being bad or doing something wrong.

This belief and story—that you did something wrong—can create a pattern in your life in which you pick relationships where your partner leaves or there is some other unwanted outcome. This is a story that, sadly, I see time and time again.

Another person may have the same experience but didn't think they did anything wrong and knew that it wasn't about them. Whatever the reason—perhaps because of the way their parents communicated about it or other situational circumstances—that person wouldn't have the same experience in adulthood because they didn't have the same underlying story.

Understanding and having intellectual knowledge that you didn't do anything wrong isn't enough to change the pattern. We must really know and feel something in our gut and subconscious to actually make the change. Intellectual knowledge will only take you so far. It is the subconscious mind that is really running the show.

That is where the belief or story—that you are not good enough or you are not worthy—lives. When we have a belief, our subconscious mind attracts people and circumstances to prove it is true. Of course, this is not a conscious decision. Remember, it is the subconscious running the show and attracting a relationship that proves to you that you aren't worthy for the other person to stay and treat you with respect.

As I continued working with people, I focused on pinpointing the belief and using spiritual practices to shift it. The belief is what the story is created out of. If I have a belief that I am stupid, I may create a story that says, "I can't be successful. I will never be able to support myself." My actions would match the story, and I might never try to pursue the education or work toward the career that I felt required intelligence. This creates a vicious cycle that continues to repeat itself again and again until we shift the belief.

Throughout my work, I saw that although the process of shifting the belief with spiritual practice worked, getting to the belief took time. Some beliefs are so deeply ingrained in the subconscious that uncovering them requires a lot of digging.

After about two years of being a spiritual practitioner, I saw Dr. Brian

Weiss, a psychiatrist who used hypnosis with his patients, on the *Oprah Winfrey Show*. As he was regressing a patient to the source of her anxiety, she ended up going to a past life. Her life was different in terms of where and how she lived. However, in exploring the true source of her anxiety, Dr. Weiss was able to support her in shifting her subconscious and relieving the anxiety. This was the beginning of his work around past-life regression.

I was riveted by his story and devoured his books. I trained in a small group with him to learn how to do hypnosis and past-life regression. He encouraged us to obtain more training in hypnosis and hypnotherapy to further support us in doing the work. That is exactly what I did.

I came across the Wellness Institute's program, "Heart-Centered Hypnotherapy," and completed their intensive program, followed by a two-year internship and three years in their Mentors program.

After completing the "Heart-Centered Hypnotherapy" training, hypnotherapy has become a vital component of the work I do. In hypnosis, we have direct access to the subconscious mind and can make a shift in consciousness. And that is when things really change.

Consciousness precedes form; therefore, shifting our consciousness shifts our experience. While in a trance state, we can identify the source of the false or limiting belief. We then change it at the source, which leads to lasting change.

Cindy came to me with an intense fear of swimming and no knowledge of an experience that would contribute to the fear. In hypnosis, I instructed her to go to the source of the fear. She was two years old, in a pool with her dad. She briefly slipped out of his arms and went under. He quickly pulled her out. While she was under, she heard her mother scream, and this created panic in her. She believed something horrible had happened and that she wasn't safe in the water. While still in a trance, I guided her to connect with her two-year-old self and provided comfort, reassuring her that she was safe and protected. After working together for a period of time, she was able to go in the water and feel safe and confident.

Over the years, I have developed my own unique way of combining hypnotherapy, spiritual practices, and other modalities to create Heart Shift. By using the key components in Heart Shift, I can create an individualized, flexible path for each client based on what they are working through, their personal belief system, readiness, and receptivity.

In the following chapters, you will see examples of how this works and how people have experienced Heart Shift and rewritten their stories to live a more fulfilling and happy life. Although the stories are all different and the people have unique backgrounds and experiences, you will see some common threads. I have found self-love to be one of the main components of having the life you desire. Loving oneself comes from trusting yourself and knowing that you choose what is true and right for you—to know that you are worth it, that you deserve to be loved, to love others, and to have a joyous life regardless of how you grew up or have experienced life thus far. That is self-love.

Oftentimes, people confuse self-love with selfishness. This could not be further from the truth. When we genuinely love ourselves, it must be the highest and best for all concerned because we are all connected. We are all one.

Let's say, for example, you were asked to help a friend move one weekend. Perhaps you had already planned something else, were going to spend time with your family, or had committed to doing some work that supports what you do in the world. You may think that dropping those plans and saying yes to helping your friend is the right thing to do, and in some cases, it may be. In other cases, the right thing is taking care of yourself. You are not required to break plans—even ones with yourself—to appease someone else.

When you allow yourself to have downtime, you recharge your battery and become more energetically available to yourself and others. Think of it this way: saying no to someone is the opportunity for you to say yes to something else! And that "something else" may have a much greater impact not only on your life but on the lives of others as well. Whether it's livelihood for your family, touching lives through your work, or spending valuable time with your loved ones, there is a deeper connection and shared love that is priceless.

This is not to say that we shouldn't help a friend in need. It is simply a reminder to pause for a moment and ask yourself what is in the highest good for who you are and who you are here to be. That is self-love.

Much of the pain I witness in my clients and in the world, in general, stems from living in the past or the future. In truth, the only time to live is now. That does not mean that the past hasn't impacted our experience of the present. As a matter of fact, it's often the past that I explore with clients to understand its impact so we can then shift it. When we dwell in the past for reasons other than learning from it to improve our present, we only hurt ourselves.

Reliving hurtful experiences of the past energetically brings our emotions into that space of hurt and pain. This draws more hurt and pain into our lives. You will see examples of this and how to let it go in some of the stories that follow.

When we focus on the future in terms of worry and concern, it can create anxiety and a space where we're so focused on figuring out what's next that we don't enjoy the moment. Anxiety and worry are different from planning for the future or having a vision of what we're creating. It's useful to have a vision because it can be a guidepost for what you're doing now. Having a clear vision allows us to ask ourselves the question: Is what I'm doing supporting my vision or detracting from it?

Living in the future with anxiety and worry and thinking, "I'll be happy when this or that happens," only prevents us from being present and seeing the beauty and joy all around us.

I support my clients in clarifying the overarching vision for their lives, overcoming the obstacles to the vision, and setting intentions based on it. When our intentions and corresponding actions are based on a clear vision, the plan set in motion is coherent and more easily followed.

To support you in applying some of the practices referred to, you will see journal prompts like the one below at the end of chapters. I encourage you to reflect on these questions and write about them. When we take pen to paper, something shifts and we can tap into our subconscious in a different way.

Journal prompt

Reflect on an event in your life that prompted you to seek change or assistance.

- What was this moment, and how did it influence your path?

Chapter 2
Why Heart Shift Matters Now

WE ARE LIVING in a time when Heart Shift is sorely needed. Many people have lost their jobs, homes, and livelihoods due to the pandemic and other economic concerns. The stress of life has taken its toll on many of us.

Alex, having notable skills and unwavering dedication, often found himself in a recurring pattern of career choices that left much to be desired. Each job began with a surge of optimism, but this initial enthusiasm quickly dissipated, leading to a sense of dissatisfaction and disillusionment. He was desperate to stop this pattern.

In our work together, Alex uncovered a hidden fear of failure that led him to choose jobs he was overqualified for, causing him to become bored and uninspired. He also had a deep need for parental approval, which played a significant role in his decisions, often leading him to prioritize their expectations over his own aspirations. In identifying his beliefs—*I can't let my parents down* and *If I go for something big, I may fail*—he was able to use the Heart Shift pillars to change them.

The U.S. Department of Labor statistics show that civilian employment dropped by 21 million from the fourth quarter of 2019 to the second quarter of 2020, and the unemployment rate more than tripled, from 3.6% to 13.0%.[1]

In March and April 2020, mental health claims for 13- to 18-year-olds almost doubled compared to the same months in the previous year.[2]

No corner of the world was left unaffected by the pandemic. The World Health Organization (WHO) states:

"One of the biggest global crises in generations, the COVID-19 pandemic has had severe and far-reaching repercussions for health systems, economies, and societies. Countless people have died or lost their livelihoods. Families and communities have been strained and separated. Children and young people have missed out on learning and socializing. Businesses have gone bankrupt. Millions of people have fallen below the poverty line. As people grapple with these health, social, and economic impacts, mental health has been widely affected. Plenty of us became more anxious, but for some, COVID-19 has sparked or amplified much more serious mental health problems."[3]

Want to learn more? See the resources at the end of the book.

Heart Shifts aren't only transformational, enabling people to live their truest lives—they are also desperately needed in today's world.

There are literally millions of people in the world right now who are in pain and suffering mentally and emotionally.

- According to the WHO, approximately one in four people globally will experience a mental health issue in their lifetime.
- In 2020, the COVID-19 pandemic had a significant impact on mental health, with one in three people worldwide reporting anxiety and depression, according to a study published in *The Lancet*.
- A study published in the *Journal of Abnormal Psychology* found that rates of anxiety and depression have increased by 70% in the U.S. over the past 25 years.

Many of these people do not know where to turn for help. They are desperate to stop the repetition of painful patterns in failed relationships and careers, to stop feeling unworthy, not good enough, and hopeless. It's as if they have fallen into a well of despair with no way out.

Therapists and counselors have waiting lists, and costs can be prohibitive, with insurance often providing little assistance. When someone is already in a state of anxiety or depression, the search for help can feel daunting.

I envision a world where individuals wholeheartedly embrace personal responsibility, making intentional decisions that foster growth, healing, and well-being, both for themselves and others. It's crucial to emphasize that this is not about placing blame on those who are victims of circumstance. This vision respects the reality that many people face situations genuinely beyond their control—such as systemic inequities or unforeseen calamities—and it's not about holding them culpable for those conditions. It is about empowering individuals to take constructive actions within their control, aimed at improving their lives and, by extension, making a positive difference in society.

One of the things we have control over is our reaction. Newton's Third Law states, "For every action in nature, there is an equal and opposite reaction." This law is a fundamental principle of physics and serves as a compelling metaphor for the interconnectedness and balance of life. It accentuates the importance of mindfulness in our actions. What we put out in the world will come back to us, whether positive or negative. The choices we make in our words and actions matter.

The question then arises: What are you going to do with what life throws at you?

For example, let's say your spouse comes home from work angry and takes it out on you by starting an argument. You can argue and allow things to escalate, or you can look at the situation and see that they're hurting and lashing out as a release.

Now, I'm not saying that's a healthy way to release anger or suggesting that such behavior is acceptable in a relationship. What I am saying is that how you respond to your spouse's reaction will impact what happens next. When you can stay in your power rather than react negatively, chances are things will go much smoother. Of course, if there is physical aggression or frequent unprovoked arguments, that could be a reason to leave a relationship. Physical and emotional abuse are never to be tolerated.

Or let's say money is tight, and you're living paycheck to paycheck. You have not only yourself but a family to support, and you lose your job. This can feel devastating; it can literally break someone. Yet, even in this, there is a choice. Certainly, there may be a moment (or more) of tears, anger, or intense fear. But as you move through that, a shift to solution-based thinking can occur. Who can you reach out to for support? How can you go about finding a new job, getting a loan—whatever might be needed?

Action cures fear. At times, it can seem nearly impossible to act; however, once we do, the impact can be huge.

There is a way to shift. There is a way to make a change that is permanent. In the stories that follow, you will see how, through the Heart Shift process, people have changed the trajectory of their lives. There is hope and a possibility for something different—something more, something greater than your current experience.

Below are the seven pillars which, along with hypnotherapy and other modalities, comprise Heart Shift:

- **Visioning & Intention Setting:** An exploration of the deepest desires of your heart around the life you would like to live.
- **Forgiveness:** Understanding the true meaning of forgiveness and discovering how to embrace it.
- **Meditation:** What it is and how it supports consciousness shifts.
- **Trust:** What it means to trust in life and yourself.
- **Visualization:** How to bring your desires to life.
- **Affirmation:** The power of your words and how to use them.
- **Self-Love:** What it is and how to embody it (it's more than just pampering yourself with spa treatments).

These pillars are not necessarily linear. I move through them with clients based on what they are experiencing. Part 2 of this book will provide more insight into the pillars.

In Part 3, you will read client stories and see Heart Shift in action. To honor privacy, names and details have been changed, and occasionally, stories have been woven together to maintain anonymity.

Additionally, you will have access to an online book portal with worksheets, hypnosis audio, and more.

Ready? Let's dive in.

Journal prompt

Reflect on how recent events—globally, locally, or personally—have shaped your life over the past few years.

- What impacts have these experiences had on your daily existence and worldview?
- If you were to seek support, what forms of assistance and understanding would be most beneficial, and how would you prefer to receive this support?

PART II

Chapter 3

Visioning and Intention Setting

**"Knowing what you desire to experience
and how you desire to be, serves as
your guide to achieving it."**

WHEN I FIRST began to see clients as a spiritual practitioner, I had some ideas about what I wanted it to look like. I imagined praying with people after the service and having one-on-one sessions to dig deeper with them. As I reflect on that time, I realize that my ideas were actually quite limited. While all of this was positive, it wasn't until I started the practice of visioning that I realized how much more I could do by getting in touch with the higher vision for my life as a spiritual practitioner.

Visioning, simply put, is the practice of activating an energy of unconditional love around yourself, asking a series of empowering questions, and tuning into your higher consciousness for the answers.

Once a week for six months, a colleague and I would vision for our professional practices. As the weeks went on, a theme began to emerge: I saw myself with a thriving private practice that included teaching and speaking. The vision had me in a cozy, welcoming office, witnessing transformation in my clients. I imagined myself teaching large groups of people and speaking in packed auditoriums. It a vision that exceeded my expectations, and I wasn't sure I was up to the task.

Initially, the idea of teaching and speaking in front of groups made me quite nervous. As a kid, I was painfully shy and barely spoke in class. As time passed, I became comfortable with this new vision. I went from feeling self-conscious about stepping onto a stage to feeling confident and alive! I knew that was where I was meant to be. Having someone by my side during the visioning process who believed in me was very beneficial.

In sharing our visions, I sheepishly said, "I see myself on a stage speaking."

"That's what I saw too!" she exclaimed.

Visioning and intention setting are powerful tools that will support you in living a life in which you thrive. They give you clarity about what you desire to experience and how you desire to be, which will serve as your guide to achieving it. As you make choices, you can ask yourself, "Which choice is in alignment with my intention?"

The actual process of visioning that I will be sharing was developed by Rev. Michael Bernard Beckwith, Founder and Spiritual Leader of Agape International Spiritual Center. I use this process when developing a new class or program.

Visioning helped me clarify my purpose for writing this book. I heard the words "write a book" and saw myself at a book signing. I also saw myself speaking at a conference and then signing books. After further visioning, the purpose of the book—to reach and support a larger audience—became clear, as did the format for the book. This clarity provided direction and focus, making the writing process more efficient and effective. It also helped me remain motivated whenever life seemed to get in the way of my writing.

I like to think of this direction and focus as my higher why. When something feels challenging, being aware of the higher why makes it much easier to push through.

For example, navigating the journey of medical school calls for a profound connection to the higher why. The schooling is undeniably intense, stretching physical, mental, and emotional abilities. Yet, for a student who has been deeply moved by a personal experience—perhaps witnessing a loved one being cared for by a compassionate physician or nurse—the path becomes clear. This memory fuels their drive, serving as a beacon of light during the most challenging times. They are not merely learning; they are preparing to give back and provide the same care and comfort they, or their loved one, received.

When the vision came through for what my practice could look like—including teaching and speaking—it spoke to my higher why of becoming a spiritual practitioner in the first place. My life had been changed by the teachings I learned and the people who supported me along the way, and I had a deep desire to be that teacher to others. It spoke to the desire I had in high school to become a therapist or counselor. This higher why pushed me past the fear of being seen and being a leader.

I have also seen visioning work for my clients. Take Steven, for example, who is successful with a stable career. Although he wasn't unhappy with his work, he wasn't happy either. As a financial analyst, he produced valuable information and insight for those he worked for. That insight had a significant impact on the firm's clients. He knew the work mattered, and yet, without a direct connection to the people who benefited from his work, he was left feeling uninspired and dissatisfied. He had a sense that there was something more he was meant to do on this planet.

During our sessions, we discussed his skills, preferences, and desires, yet there was no clear picture of how to proceed. This is when we turned to visioning. By guiding him into a meditative state, he realized that he could fulfill his desire to help people by using his natural intuitive skills. Recognizing that this was his true calling brought him immense joy.

As we continued to engage in the visioning process over several weeks, the vision gradually got clearer. He saw an image of himself working with someone as a coach, sharing his inner wisdom in a way that supported his clients in achieving their goals. Steven's energy soared at the thought of being able to directly communicate with and support people, which was very different from his work as a financial analyst.

With his vision in mind, he set intentions that included educational pursuits, networking, and continued visioning. With his intentions set, Steven is well on his path to realizing his vision. He has completed his certification program and is currently building his professional practice as a coach!

Visioning can also provide clarity if you are overwhelmed with ideas for the future but don't know where to start. Take Kristi, for example, who was flooded with ideas for what she wanted to accomplish as the new year approached. After walking into my office, she was quick to rattle them off one after another: write a book, take up photography, start a blog, sign up for a cooking class, find a fun way to be active, and more!

She was grateful when I told her about the practice of visioning and how it could help guide her. I noticed her facial expression shift from a clenched jaw and furrowed brow to a relaxed smile as she leaned back in her chair and took a long, deep breath. We kept the process very general, focusing on the highest vision for her life in the new year. The practice helped her focus on the main things she wanted to accomplish—write a children's book and prioritize a greater emphasis on self-care.

Kristi was very successful in her career as a graphic designer and invested a lot of time in her work. The thought of taking time away felt nearly impossible. As she allowed the vision for her book to pull her forward, the old excuses—no time, it will take too long, it's not any good—started to fade away. Her higher why for writing the book became clear: to calm young children with anxiety. It was something very near and dear to her heart, as she had struggled with anxiety as a child.

With this new clarity, time seemed to expand. She set intentions for herself regarding a timeline for finishing the book and felt a renewed sense of purpose and momentum.

The visioning practice consists of entering a meditative state where you tune into your higher self and ask specific questions. It is a process of listening and observing. Note that this practice is distinct from visualization, which involves having a specific idea of what we desire and actively visualizing it. I'll explain the practice of visualization in more detail in a later chapter.

When doing the visioning process, one must be sure to:

- Listen
- Remain open and receptive
- Let go of judgment
- Not worry about the "how." The process is all about the "what."
- Recognize that the vision may come in the form of color, feeling, words, or images. Simply make a note of what comes up.

Questions to ask during visioning:

1. What is the highest vision (or divine idea) for ______________?
2. What must I release to manifest this vision?
3. What must I embrace, embody, and become to empower this vision?
4. Is there anything else I need to know right now regarding this vision?

In the book portal (linked later in the chapter), I have included a worksheet and recording to guide you through the process and experience visioning yourself. It is a process you can repeat to help clarify your purpose and priorities and take intentional action that aligns with your values and vision. By keeping the focus on your vision, you can more easily stay motivated and overcome obstacles along the way toward realizing your vision.

By tapping into our higher self and tuning into that inner voice, we harness the power of visioning. Instead of getting bogged down in the details of how to achieve something, we can focus on the "what" and the emotions and sensations it evokes within us. This allows us to be more open to new and innovative ideas.

I suggest writing down whatever comes up during a visioning session. Sometimes, something will come up that doesn't seem to make sense. Write it down anyway. A client of mine had an image of a little red sports car. It was a vivid image and, to her in that moment, made no sense. The feeling, however, was clear: when she saw the sports car, she was filled with excitement and adventure.

Several weeks later, she had an opportunity to travel to Africa with a group of friends. It had never occurred to her to go there before, and when it came up, she felt the excitement and adventure she'd had when she envisioned the little red sports car.

She said yes to the trip, and it proved to be an amazing experience. She went on a safari where she saw leopards, mongooses, and black herons, took a boat down the Rufiji River, and enjoyed the beach in Zanzibar. Had she not seen that little red sports car in her vision and tuned into the excitement and adventure, she might not have said yes to that trip.

Visioning is a practice, and it is essential to remember the key word: practice. The first time you try it, you may or may not get much, and that is okay—simply keep practicing. When I first became involved at the spiritual center, I was asked to be on the Visioning Core. I had never experienced the visioning process and didn't know what to expect. We were a group of 6 to 8 people who met regularly to vision for the spiritual center and its future growth.

The first time we visioned together, I got nothing. I was reassured by the group leader that this was not unusual. As time went on, I had incredible experiences of seeing, feeling, and hearing things. One time, I heard, *focus on love and service.* Those words not only helped the center but also impacted the way I work with people. Another time, I saw people coming together to share a meal. For me, this symbolized community building, which was a big part of our focus. I predominantly perceive words and phrases, some of which I'd never use or say. This validated that the vision originated in my higher self rather than my intellect.

I first heard *write a book* back in 2013. At the time, and for some time after that, I couldn't imagine doing so. I struggled to see what I could possibly say that would matter to people. Of course, it wasn't about the *how*, only the *what*, which was *write a book*. There were several other points in time when I heard during visioning that I was to write a book. It wasn't until 2022, while at a Thought Leader Academy Conference, that the vision to write a book and share stories of hope with others began to take hold.

Consider an aspect of your life that could benefit from having a clear vision. It could be your relationship with a partner, your career, or anything you are working on. Grab a notebook or journal, find a quiet spot, and listen to the guided visioning in the book portal. Allow yourself time to simply be in the process and watch what happens. I suggest visioning once or twice a week for several weeks and saving your notes. After you have done this for a few weeks, review all your notes and notice the themes and similarities. As you identify the themes, pay particular attention to what they look and feel like. Spending time in meditation and contemplating these themes can help solidify the vision. Connecting with the vision energetically draws it to you in terms of action steps that come to you intuitively.

Remember, visioning is about tuning into the *what*, trusting you will be guided to the *how*.

Happy visioning!

Would you like guidance on visioning? Learn more in the book portal, where you can download a worksheet for note-taking and play the recording of me guiding you through it. Access the portal here:

Or go to:
https://www.joancoletto.com/heart-shift-book-portal

Remember to write down whatever comes up, even if it doesn't seem to make sense. Pay attention to words, emotions, and images. When we engage in regular visioning, a pattern often reveals itself. I have included the written version of the process for your reference.

Guided Visioning Process:

Make sure that you are in a comfortable place as you begin this process. Remain open and receptive as you listen without judgment. This process is about catching the vision for what, not how. Ensure you have something to write with. The vision may come through by way of feelings, words, images, or colors. Make a note of whatever arises, regardless of whether it seems to make sense or not.

Begin by focusing on your breath. Feel the breath entering your body, perhaps noticing it entering through your nose, making its way into your chest, moving into your abdomen, and then releasing slowly through your mouth. Allow yourself to feel the rhythmic nature of the breath.

Now, begin to place your attention on your heart. You might imagine that you're inhaling and exhaling through your heart as you activate the energy in your heart chakra. Focus your breath and energy on your heart, feeling it gently open as you access all the loving energy within. There is an infinite amount of loving energy within your heart. It is your connection to Source, and there is always more than enough.

Know that you are connected to all of life, to the universe, and that as you ask, you receive. Know that right now, right here, you are an open channel, receiving the wisdom of the universe. You are in a place of hearing with the inner ear and seeing with the inner eye.

Remember that you are not concerned with *how* as you vision. You are simply concerned with *what*.

Take a deep breath, and from this place of deep connection with the universe and with all life, ask:

1. What is the highest vision (or divine idea) for _____________________?
2. What must I release in order to manifest this vision?

3. What must I embrace, embody, and become to empower this vision?
4. Is there anything else I need to know right now regarding this vision?

Journal prompt

- How does having or not having a vision impact your daily experiences and long-term aspirations?

Chapter 4

Forgiveness

**"Forgiveness is letting go so the past
doesn't hold you prisoner."**

MY FIRST MARRIAGE gave me many opportunities to practice forgiveness. As I began my spiritual journey following my divorce, I realized that I was still holding onto the pain of deceit, unfulfilled expectations, and the ending of what I thought was my forever relationship. I thought forgiveness was somehow saying that the things he did didn't matter and that forgiving him was letting him off the hook. I didn't yet understand that forgiveness was not about my former husband; it was about me.

In practicing forgiveness, I was able to see my part in the relationship. I was young—only 20 years old when we married—and I didn't really know myself. I had never lived on my own and was uncertain what I wanted out of life. Getting married and feeling a sense of independence sounded exciting, so I went forward without fully considering the magnitude of that decision. I remember my father walking me down the aisle, wearing the same white wedding gown my mother wore, and thinking, *What am I doing? Why am I doing this?* Something in me said, *This is not right,* yet I could not stop what had been set in motion.

By holding onto that pain and blaming my former husband, I was only hurting myself. He could go on living his life in any manner he chose—in joy, in pain, or anything in between. The only thing I had true dominion over was my life and how I chose to live.

When I realized this, through one of my mentors at the spiritual center, I began my personal journey of forgiveness. Yogi Bhajan said, "If you want to learn something, read about it. If you want to understand something, write about it. If you want to master something, teach it." This is exactly what I set out to do.

After doing quite a bit of reading and journaling about it, I decided it was time to share my experience and what I learned. For the next three years, I hosted a weekly "Forgiveness Friday" conference call. The call consisted of teaching about what forgiveness truly is: releasing resentment, anger, and other negative emotions. I'd describe how those feelings take on a significant emotional toll, and by releasing them, you free yourself from the bondage you've been experiencing. After holding space for people to share their thoughts if they felt inspired to do so, I'd then guide them through a meditation or visualization practice, several of which can be found in the book portal.

Hosting that weekly call had a profound impact on my level of forgiveness. I was able to think of my former husband or even remember a particular situation that previously brought up a lot of pain and I felt completely neutral about it. The sadness and anger that used to overwhelm me had dissolved. When we hold onto unforgiveness and relive past moments of hurt and pain, we become attached to that person or situation. It is like there is an invisible cord attaching you to that person. Forgiveness will set you free.

When Debby came to me, she was struggling with intimate relationships. The partners she repeatedly chose were unfaithful, and she was not only suffering from the infidelity, but she was also holding onto the pain by reliving the stories and circumstances over and over in her mind. She had not found a way to let go and begin to move on.

When we continue to replay a story like this, we tend to bring more of it into our lives. The stories we repeatedly tell ourselves become ingrained in the subconscious mind, and then we attract more of the same. This is why understanding these subconscious patterns and behaviors and shifting them at the level of the subconscious is vital in making a true and permanent shift.

Debby's story was: *All men cheat, and it is an unforgivable offense.* Now, I'm not suggesting that when two people agree to be monogamous, cheating is acceptable in any way. Forgiveness is not saying that what the other person did is acceptable; it's about letting go of the resentment so that you can move on and live your life.

Using hypnosis, I regressed Debby back to the source of the pain she experienced around men cheating. Her father had cheated on her mother. While she knew this had happened, she didn't realize she was still holding onto resentment toward her father. She blamed him for the end of her parents' marriage and the big changes that happened after their divorce. Throughout her childhood, she split her time between two homes that were not in close proximity to each other. Suddenly, she went from seeing her friends every weekend to every few weeks. The isolation and negative feelings she was holding onto caused her to become quieter and more withdrawn, and her grades suffered.

While the cheating was a catalyst, there was a lot that went on between her parents before, during, and after that led to the divorce. She didn't have all the facts about what happened, and it wasn't really her place to know.

What she learned through Heart Shift was that blaming her father for the divorce was only creating more of the same story in her life. Forgiveness was the key to Debby attracting the kind of relationship she deeply desired.

In moving through the forgiveness process, Debby has built a stronger, more loving relationship with her father. This did not happen overnight. It happened over the course of several months, with some bumps along the way. One of those bumps was that her relationship with her mother got a little rocky as she stopped seeing her mother as a victim. This presented an opportunity to do some forgiveness work around her mother as well, and their relationship has also grown stronger.

The key requirement to begin the process of forgiveness is a willingness to release blame and embrace responsibility. The level of difficulty in doing this depends on a couple of factors. First, is it a minor transgression or a life-changing circumstance that you're looking to forgive? And how long have you been holding onto the unforgiveness? The longer we have been holding onto it, the more challenging it can be to finally forgive. This is where willingness comes in.

If someone is not willing to begin, I take some time to explore how forgiveness could directly impact their life. What are the specific circumstances they're experiencing as a result of unforgiveness? What might be different if they let go and allowed forgiveness to set them free? Sometimes, one must experience a certain degree of pain before one becomes willing to do the work it takes to forgive.

While working with clients on forgiveness, I take them through a four-step process. You will find a worksheet in the book portal to support you through your forgiveness journey.

Step #1: Feel and express all your feelings

Being heard is a deep desire we have as human beings. In the case of forgiveness work, we typically want the one who has wronged us to hear us. Often, this is simply not possible, and even if they did hear the words, they may not actually get what we are saying. Being able to let it all out still matters, even if it's simply speaking it aloud and admitting it to yourself or telling a trusted friend who is willing to listen. If speaking to someone and telling the story is not an option, you can write it down. Write about it in the most unenlightened, blaming way—let it all out.

As you express yourself, it is crucial to be aware of the story you've attached to the circumstance or person you intend to forgive. It is the story that provides the real opportunity for healing and release.

As you are telling your story, either verbally or in writing, you will most likely notice emotions coming up—anger, fear, sadness. Notice whatever it is and allow yourself to feel it. We hold emotions in our bodies. When you are nervous, you may feel a fluttering in your stomach.

When angry, there may be pressure building in your head. When sad, there may be an ache in your chest. Allow the emotions to move through and out with a physical action. You may have been taught that yelling or stomping your feet is inappropriate, so it can feel wrong. I am not suggesting that you do this in front of a room full of people; however, finding a safe space to release the emotion is key to the first step in freedom from the pain. Exercise can also be a great way to release the emotions from your body. It is amazing to me how effective yelling into a pillow can be! Give it a try sometime and see for yourself.

Debby shared her story: "Dad doesn't love me." "He left me because I am not worth staying for." As she yelled into the pillow, she got louder and louder, the anger rising along with the volume of her voice. "If I were smarter, prettier, nicer, he would have stayed." "Nobody wants me. I will never be enough." She buried her face in the pillow and sobbed. These are the stories that supported her belief that all men cheat.

Step #2: Break it down to only the facts

This can sometimes be a little tough. When I am working with a client on this step, I often have to ask questions like, Can you be sure [name of person felt [emotion]? Or if someone had been there observing, would they have seen or heard it exactly that way?

We all have our own narratives about the events in our lives. Set aside whatever you felt in the moment and whatever you came to believe about the person or situation and break it down to just the facts. Writing down the facts can help because seeing them in print often makes it easier to break things down. Remember, while I said it was simple—it is not necessarily easy.

Let's say you have a friend who you feel is judging your parenting. You're at a restaurant, and your little one is sitting in her highchair eating. In the middle of lunch, she starts to melt down and scream. You try everything—more food, toys, taking her out of the highchair. Your friend says something like, "I would never allow my child to behave that way. I would teach her to have good manners."

You bristle. You make a remark (or not), all the while fuming at her insensitivity. *I can't believe she actually said that! What does she know anyway? She's not a parent.*

Now, what are the facts? Your child is becoming loud, and your friend said, "I would never allow my child to behave that way. I would teach her to have good manners." That is it. Anything else is your personal narrative.

When Debby broke it down to the facts as she knew them, it had nothing to do with her. Her father broke his commitment to her mother. He entered a relationship with another woman and ended the marriage. Although he wasn't living in the same home with Debby, he never failed to pick her up when it was his time with her. He attended her activities when parents were invited, and when he wasn't with her, he called to check in on her frequently. This was all eye-opening to Debby, as she had never considered these facts before. Her focus was solely on what he didn't do, which was live in the home with her.

Step #3: Flip It

What if the opposite of my narrative is true? Who is really to say what is true? Facts are facts, and stories are judgments. Based on the facts, imagine how your narrative could shift. Take some time to consider the possibility. You cannot really know what someone else is feeling or thinking. You cannot know their motivation either. We all come from different backgrounds and see life through the lens of our own experiences.

Using the example above of the friend judging your parenting in the restaurant, imagine how it would be if you flipped it. Perhaps her remark was her way of trying to be helpful. Maybe she was masking her own discomfort. What if you shrugged it off, recognizing that no one can know what they would do in a particular situation unless they are in it? Most parents have had a similar moment of dealing with a screaming child and know not to judge.

In Debby's case, she began to consider the possibility that perhaps her father was very unhappy in the marriage. Perhaps there were things going on between her parents that she was unaware of. While lying and cheating are not constructive ways to solve a problem, perhaps he didn't know of another way.

Debby was able to see his humanity and understand that perhaps he didn't mean to hurt anyone—he simply wanted to soothe his own pain. She also recognized the effort that he made to stay connected to her and be the best father he could be.

Step #4: Own It

Take full responsibility for your part. Depending on the situation, it may or may not be appropriate to have a conversation. When we free ourselves by forgiving, sometimes a relationship can become stronger. Sometimes, it ends. And sometimes, it simply shifts a bit. You may be inclined to set some boundaries in a relationship, whether verbalized or not.

In the example of the friend judging parenting, you may want to have a conversation with your friend at a later time, expressing your frustration in that moment of not being able to calm your child. It might go something like this:

"When you said you'd never let your child behave that way, I felt judged at a time when I was feeling insecure and needed support."

Based on her response, you might add:

"What I really needed was for you to help me by trying to distract her or even suggesting we go somewhere else."

Additionally, you might also discuss how you could both handle something like this in the future. This is where honestly owning your part and being vulnerable can really strengthen and deepen a relationship.

Although this example is fairly simple, the steps to forgiveness are consistent. It all comes down to the one thing in life we have dominion over: ourselves. We choose who to surround ourselves with, how to behave in certain situations, what matters most, what we want out of life, and so forth. Forgiveness provides the opportunity for growth, and as we harvest the learning from challenges in our lives, we grow stronger and more capable of living in joy.

Debby was able to have a very healing conversation with her father. She owned her part in the way she pulled back from him in her teen years and rejected his efforts to be close. She shared that she blamed him not only for moving out but also for the change in her mother, who had become bitter and less emotionally available to Debby. Rather than enjoy the time she did have with him, she pushed him away as punishment. She now understood she was also punishing herself and that his extra-marital affair was not a reflection of how he felt about her. Her father also shared his disappointment in himself for not handling things better and for making it hard on Debby. He shared that if he had worked on the issues within the marriage, he might not have sought out a relationship outside the marriage.

Her relationship with her mother, although close, is something she is still working on. She had hoped to have a meaningful conversation with her and share some of what she had shared with her father. Her mother is still holding onto a lot of anger and resentment toward her ex-husband and is not open to that level of connection. Debby knows that forgiveness is not always easy. She is grateful for the freedom she has experienced and hopes one day her mother will feel the same. In the meantime, she is not allowing her mother's lack of forgiveness toward her father to have a negative impact on their relationship.

You will find a forgiveness worksheet in the book portal, along with several guided meditations to support you on your forgiveness journey. I invite you to practice forgiveness, starting with something small. When you apply these steps to a situation that isn't highly emotionally charged, you'll gain a clear understanding of how the process functions, thereby having the ability to more easily apply it in highly charged circumstances. Remember, it is a practice and can take time. I assure you, it is worth the effort.

To deepen your journey with this chapter, I invite you to explore the guided meditations and complete the forgiveness worksheet, all available on the book portal. You can also follow the meditation script here in the book if you prefer.

4 Steps to Forgiveness Worksheet

1. **Feel and express all your feelings through telling your story.** Let it all out including the judgements and criticism.
2. **Break it down to only the facts.** If someone was observing the situation, what would they have seen and heard?
3. **Flip it.** What if the opposite of your story was true? Look at the facts and tell a different story.
4. **Own it.** Take full responsibility for whatever might have been your part.

Remember, when using these steps, start with something small so that you can experience how it works. When it comes to long-standing unforgiveness or deeply painful situations, the process can take some time, and it is often helpful in those cases to have support during the process.

Forgiveness Meditations

These meditations are designed to support you as you go through the four steps of forgiveness.

Listening to the recordings of the meditations in the book portal will allow you to fully experience them.

Meditation #1

A Buddhist meditation for forgiveness. This is a very gentle way to begin a forgiveness practice.

Allow yourself to be in a comfortable position and gently close your eyes. Bring your attention to your heart center, in the middle of your chest. Allow yourself to feel whatever is there without any judgment.

Breathe through your heart, and imagine that as you say the words below, you are saying them through your heart.

Think of the ways you have harmed yourself and harmed others. It is best to begin with minor things, not the big acts of harming. To whatever degree you are able, extend forgiveness to yourself for this harm by saying these phrases to yourself or out loud:

- I allow myself to be imperfect.
- I allow myself to make mistakes.
- I allow myself to be a learner, still learning life lessons.
- I forgive myself. If I cannot forgive myself now, may I forgive myself sometime in the future.

Think of the ways others have harmed you, again beginning with minor harms. As much as you are able, extend forgiveness to them.

- Just as I allow myself to be imperfect, so I allow you to be imperfect.
- I also allow you to make mistakes.
- I allow you to be a learner, still learning life lessons.
- I forgive you. If I cannot forgive you now, may I forgive you sometime in the future.

Now, ask for forgiveness from others for the harm that you have done to them.

- Please allow me to be imperfect.
- Please allow me to make mistakes.
- Please allow me to be a learner, still learning life lessons.
- If you cannot forgive me now, please try to forgive me sometime in the future.

Allow yourself to take a few deep breaths. Notice how you feel. What are your emotions and thoughts after speaking these words? Take some time to journal your experience.

Meditation #2

Allow yourself to be in a comfortable place, free from distractions. Take a few minutes to simply focus on your breath, allowing yourself to become grounded and centered.

Visualize yourself holding on to resentment and unforgiveness. Imagine unforgiveness as a physical weight that you are holding; include any people or situations that you have not forgiven. Now, imagine yourself walking down a path out in nature. It is a beautiful path nestled among trees and flowers. Continue walking along, carrying the weight of resentment and unforgiveness.

Eventually, you come to a footbridge. As you cross over this footbridge, you notice an image on the other side. As you get closer, you realize the image you see is you, one year from now. What do you look like? What do you feel like? Look into your eyes and notice what you observe. What is your life like?

Imagine now that you are walking on, continuing down this beautiful path, still carrying the weight of resentment and unforgiveness. After some twists and turns, you come to another footbridge. Cross over the footbridge, and again, an image appears on the other side. This time, the image is you five years from now. Notice what you look like. What is your posture? Your facial expression? What does your life look like five years from now?

As you move on, perhaps walking a little slower under the weight of resentment and unforgiveness, you come to another footbridge and cross. There you are, ten years from now! What do you see? What are the emotions and feelings? What do you look like? What is your life like?

As you move on, you begin walking down a different path. While you are on this path, release the burden of resentment and unforgiveness. Lay it down and notice how you feel. What is your posture like? What emotions do you feel? Continue down this new path without the weight and burden of resentment and unforgiveness.

This time, when you come to the footbridge, cross over it and see yourself several years from now—several years after releasing the resentment. What do you see? What are your feelings and emotions? What is your life like after releasing the burden of resentment?

Reflect on how you would like to live your life. What choices do you desire to make? Are you willing to do what it takes to forgive and let go of the resentment? Are you ready to free yourself?

Now, bring yourself back to the present by taking a few deep, cleansing breaths. Reflect on the impact that releasing resentment and embracing forgiveness can have on your life.

Meditation #3
Self-Forgiveness Meditation

Imagine a golden light all around you, enfolding you in its energy. This is a healing, protective light.

Relax, breathing deeply once or twice, allowing your entire body to feel calm and tranquil.

Imagine yourself in a beautiful garden. It is a warm, sunny day, and you are feeling good as you walk through the flowers and trees. Notice the scents and colors around you.

As you walk along, you come to a huge mirror standing in the center of this garden. Approach this mirror and look closely at your reflection. What do you see? Are you seeing someone you feel entirely comfortable with? Do you feel a sense of total, unconditional love for this person looking back at you?

Perhaps you see yourself as someone who has made many mistakes in their life. Perhaps you see guilt and shame. Perhaps you feel your self-esteem plummet, and the feeling of unworthiness pushes through. Remember the emotions you felt when you did not like the way you behaved.

Let the negative emotions that you have felt in your life break free—the blame you felt at your parents' divorce, the sadness you felt when you were left out, or the pain of feeling not good enough.

Stand and think about how you really feel about yourself as you look at yourself in the mirror.

Now, move away from the mirror and continue down the path in the garden. As you round a corner, you come upon a waterfall flowing into a lake. Step into the water and allow the waterfall to wash away all discomfort and negative feelings of unworthiness and guilt.

As the water washes over you, feel yourself become lighter and happier. A sense of deep well-being washes over you as you stand underneath this healing current of the waterfall.

Now, repeat the following out loud or to yourself:

- I love and forgive myself totally.

- I recognize that my worth is unchanging and is not increased by my success nor decreased by my mistakes.
- I choose to live in the now and not hold the past against myself.
- I choose to approve of myself; I do not need to seek approval from others.
- I love myself because I am worthy of love.

Now, I invite you to walk back to the mirror and look at the person looking back at you. Has your image changed at all? Do you feel lighter? Happier?

Now, slowly bring your awareness back to the present moment, taking a deep breath in and out.

When you are ready, you may open your eyes.

Meditation #4

Get comfortable, gently close your eyes, and focus for several minutes on your breath.

Visualize a beautiful golden box. It is a square box—rather large, with a top on it. Imagine that this box is on a table in front of you. There is light emanating from this box—a beautiful pink light—a loving, healing light.

Now, bring to your mind a situation or person who has hurt you and caused you pain. When you have an image of the situation or person, imagine the lid opening and see the thought of the situation or person being placed in the box. Let the thought go and place it in the box—empty your mind of it. Now, bring another hurt to your mind and see that thought being placed in the box. Take a few moments and allow all the people and situations you are willing to forgive to come to mind. Visualize placing them in the box.

When your mind is clear, imagine closing the lid on the box, trapping all those thoughts inside. Now, repeat after me:

"I choose to live in the now. I release all thoughts of regret, revenge, judgment, and blame. Universe, I turn all these situations and people over to you for forgiveness now."

Envision that beautiful pink light around the golden box becoming brighter and more vibrant. Know that anytime an unwanted thought comes up, you can place it in the box for forgiveness.

Take three deep, cleansing breaths and allow yourself to bring your attention to the present.

Journal prompt

- Has your definition of forgiveness shifted, and if so, how?
- If there is a relationship or situation in your life where there is an opportunity to forgive, how might forgiveness impact you?

On a scale of 1-10, how willing are you to do the forgiveness steps?

Chapter 5

Meditation

"You have the answers to all your
questions within. A solid meditation
practice will support you in listening."

RECENTLY, I FOUND myself in a challenging situation. I had to
have a procedure done on my eye to remove a small growth.
Although my eye was numb, I was completely aware during
the procedure. While lying there, I felt my palms getting sweaty, a pit
forming in my stomach, and a strong desire to be anywhere else. My
visual focus was on the upper rim of the light shining on my eye. The
antiseptic smell filled my nostrils. The thought of the doctor making
an incision in my eye was terrifying to me. I wanted to run, but I was
trapped there, completely vulnerable.

I knew I needed to calm my nervous system, so I began to breathe
deeply and focus on each breath entering my body. I concentrated on
filling my lungs and belly, then gently and fully releasing the breath. After
a few deep breaths, the pit in my stomach was gone, and my palms had
dried. I felt safe and protected.

Meditation is a mental practice that involves training the mind to focus and achieve a state of relaxation, clarity, and emotional balance. It is a technique that has been practiced for thousands of years in various cultures and traditions. Meditation can be done in many different ways, and one of the most common forms involves sitting quietly, focusing on the breath, and observing thoughts and sensations as they arise—without judgment or attachment. Through regular practice, meditation can help reduce stress and anxiety, improve concentration and focus, promote emotional stability, and cultivate a deeper sense of inner peace and overall well-being.

Meditation can be a powerful tool for improving both mental and physical health, as well as promoting a sense of calm and well-being. In addition to the benefits I have already mentioned, meditation can also improve sleep by helping you relax and stay calm. It can even boost your immune system. A study published in the *Annals of Behavioral Medicine* in 2015 found that mindfulness meditation can reduce inflammation in the body, which is linked to a wide range of health problems, including autoimmune disorders and cardiovascular disease.

I have personally found meditation to be a great benefit. Having a regular practice enables me to tap into that sense of calm when needed throughout my day. Recently, during a heated conversation with my husband, I was able to pause, take a couple of deep breaths, and tune into the outcome I wanted—peace. That simple shift changed not only my next words but also my tone of voice and posture. In turn, this influenced his reaction, and we both felt better.

Even beyond the benefits I've mentioned, meditation can also assist you in attuning to your higher self and honing your ability to hear your intuitive voice. This practice has the potential to offer guidance and focus, leading to increased clarity and direction—a core part of Heart Shift.

We each have the answers to all our questions within. My role with my clients is to ask the right questions and support them in listening to and trusting themselves. A solid foundational meditation practice aids in that listening.

While meditation and visioning are both receptive practices, they do differ. In meditation, we listen to our higher self or higher power, tuning into whatever wisdom is there for us. Many times, it is simply the process of being still, being calm, and reaping the health benefits of that state.

Visioning, on the other hand, is the practice of asking specific questions and then listening to our higher self or higher power to clarify our purpose or mission.

Consistency is a key element in establishing a meditation practice for several reasons:

- **It helps build the habit.** As with any other habit, meditation requires consistent practice to become a part of your daily routine.
- **It supports the development of concentration.** When you meditate regularly, you train your mind to focus on one thing at a time. With practice, your concentration improves, and you become more focused and present in all aspects of your life.
- **It deepens your insights and understanding of yourself and the world around you.** By observing your thoughts and emotions regularly, you gain a better understanding of your own patterns and habits and how they affect your life.
- **It cultivates a sense of calm and inner peace.** Regular meditation helps reduce stress and anxiety while increasing feelings of relaxation and tranquility.

While I do enjoy engaging in longer meditation sessions, my typical practice lasts for 15 minutes in the morning, sometimes accompanied by background music. I like to sit in an upright position, gently close my eyes, and focus on my breath. My favorite place to meditate is in my home office. I sit in a comfy chair, light a candle or incense, and wrap a shawl around my shoulders. If thoughts arise—which they sometimes do—I simply imagine them floating away, vanishing into the air. Resisting or trying to force thoughts away only serves to give them more energy.

I use the Insight Timer app, which offers both guided meditations and silent background music options. While I'm sure there are other apps that are equally effective, this one has been my go-to.

To encourage clients to be consistent, I tell them to be realistic about the amount of time they can devote to practicing. Starting with even five minutes a day can make a difference. Ultimately, working up to at least 15 minutes a day is optimal. The main thing is to start.

So how can meditation help create a Heart Shift in your life?

Despite his seemingly cheerful and lively hosting demeanor, TV host Tom Bergeron revealed that he had struggled with controlling his temper for many years. "The temper thing was always directed at inanimate objects or myself," he said. After receiving an ultimatum from his girlfriend—now wife—he sought out meditation to control his anger. Regarding meditation, he said, "It does make you happier. It does make you better able to assess things as they're happening so as not to fly off the handle. I have not damaged any Sheetrock in 35 years, I'm proud to say. It's the belief that I can be the master of how I react to any situation. It's not the situation that I should blame. Ultimately, if things go off the rails, it's how I react to it."

I encourage you to develop a meditation practice of your own. If this is new to you, begin with just five minutes a day. Committing to longer sessions right away might feel overwhelming and lead to discouragement. The idea is to make meditation a regular habit, and once established, you can slowly increase the length. You can also practice simply being more present as you move through your day—mentally noting what you see and do or taking a few conscious deep breaths periodically.

I have recorded several guided meditations that you may access through the book portal. They are of varying lengths, allowing you to choose based on the time you have available.

Journal prompt

- If you do not currently meditate regularly, how could doing so transform your life?

> • If you meditate regularly, do you anticipate making any shifts to your practice and, if so, what would they be?

Grounding Meditation

Focus your attention now on your breath, noticing your inhale, noticing your exhale. Have your feet on the floor as you're sitting, making sure that your arms and legs are uncrossed to allow the flow of energy to move through you. Feel yourself sinking into the surface that you are sitting on, allowing it to fully and completely support you as you lean into the rhythmic nature of the breath.

Imagine now that your feet are rooted in place, energetically drawn down to the earth, and in your mind's eye, create a grounding cord. You can imagine this as a sensation that drops from your first chakra at the base of your spine down into the ground. It may be a beam of light or any type of material you desire. Allow this grounding cord to go deeper and deeper, transcending whatever space you are currently in, touching the soil, and moving deep into the ground. As the cord continues to move deeper, imagine it is reaching the center of the earth. This is your grounding cord. You are always connected with it as you move through this life. It has the ability to attract anything that is not in your highest good or is not for you and pull it into the earth, allowing it to be recycled into new energy.

Using the power of your mind, begin to collect any energy in your body that is not serving you—anything that is not in your highest and best interest. Allow this energy to flow down the grounding cord and reach the center of the earth, where it is recycled and transformed.

Once you have completed sending all energy that is not for you into the earth, express appreciation to Mother Earth for recycling this energy into positive energy.

I invite you now to call back any energy that you have put out into the world. Calling back this energy allows the good that it has done to remain, as it brings the energy back for you and your highest good.

Imagine your body temple surrounded by a beautiful bubble of love, and as you feel yourself in this bubble, imagine there is an opening at the top. This opening acts as a filter, cleansing and purifying the energy you have given out so that it returns to you completely cleansed and pure. See this energy being collected and cleansed. As the energy fills your body, feel yourself becoming revitalized and re-energized. This energy has come back to you completely pure, filled with love and light. Notice the feelings of love, wholeness, and peace that this energy returns to you.

Allow yourself now to sit for several minutes in this healing energy, feeling connected, loved, and whole.

When you are complete, I invite you to take three deep, cleansing breaths. As you exhale on the third breath, open your eyes and shift around in your seat, knowing this time of meditation is complete.

Gratitude Meditation

Allow yourself to get comfortable in your seat with your arms and legs uncrossed and your back supported. Allow your eyes to gently close. Slowly inhale a full, deep breath and exhale slowly. Consciously slow your breath and focus on the breath entering your body, filling your lungs and belly, and then releasing. Release any attachments to emotions or thoughts that may arise. As a thought comes, which it probably will, simply let it go without forcing or pushing. Simply say to yourself, "I'm not interested in that right now," and let it float away as you continue taking these slow, deep breaths.

There is light and warmth in your heart. Get in touch with that heart energy. You might imagine that you're inhaling and exhaling through your heart energy. Feel the loving energy within your heart filling your body and surrounding you in this beautiful energy of love and light. While you feel this energy, you notice things that you are grateful for—the people in your life, the support you receive, the work you do in the world, your health. Sense and feel the gratitude expanding your heart. Feel the warm embrace of love, peace, and gratitude. *(Pause as long as you like.)*

Take a deep breath in and exhale completely as you begin to bring your attention back to the room. Shift around in your seat a little bit. Open your eyes and know that the love, the light, and this energy of gratitude stay with you in your heart and in your being!

Experience Being Present Meditation

Allow yourself to sit down in a comfortable position with your arms and legs uncrossed. Notice your breath going in and out. Become very aware of your breathing…

Now, reflect on the presence of the universe in the atmosphere around you. Sense the light and love of this presence as you inhale and exhale. See yourself bathed in the energy of the universe, that which permeates everything. Now, notice the sensations within your body. Notice the feeling of your skin and the touch of your clothing on your skin. Feel the sensations in your mouth and your tongue as it rests on your teeth. Notice any other bodily sensation and reflect that every sensation is the biochemical process of the energy, power, and presence that is the creative life within you.

Feel the universal power at work within you as you listen and hear the sounds of all life around you. Every sound reflects the universal action around you. Imagine opening your heart and mind to all the good things. Feel the good welling up from within you. Know that words spoken from a meditative consciousness have the power to manifest and initiate change as they wash away false limitations. Feel the wisdom within you. Listen for your intuitive voice. Know that you can follow this wisdom into action.

Now, take a deep breath, bring your attention back to the room, and open your eyes.

Chapter 6

Trust

**"Feelings of confidence and security
within support the ability to trust."**

I STAYED IN MY first marriage far longer than necessary. Deep down, at the core of my being I knew that I was making a mistake on my wedding day. I remember standing in the back of the church, about to take my father's arm to walk down the aisle, and thinking, *What am I doing? This is a mistake.* I brushed it off, smiled, and walked down the aisle.

The following years were turbulent, filled with ups and downs. I thought about leaving many times, yet I didn't trust that I could be on my own any more than I trusted myself on my wedding day.

Merriam-Webster.com defines trust as "reliance on the character, ability, strength, or truth of someone or something—one in which confidence is placed." It has been said that all trust is based on the degree of trust we have in ourselves. While I don't know if I totally agree with that statement, I do believe it holds some truth. It's possible for someone to trust themselves yet be inherently mistrustful of others due to past experiences or personal beliefs. But is that really mistrust, or is it greater caution? It's also possible for someone with little self-trust to be overly trusting of others because of their lack of confidence in their own decision-making abilities. And yet, are they really trusting or simply relinquishing responsibility for decisions?

My client, Maggie, trusted herself but not others due to past experiences. As you will see in Chapter 13, when I recount more of her story, she had been abused as a young child, and when Maggie told her mother, she did not believe her. Her mother thought she was making it up or exaggerating. This was devastating to Maggie. If her mother didn't believe her then, how could anyone else? She felt frightened and alone.

That was the moment she lost faith in others. If she couldn't trust her mother—the one person who was supposed to protect her and keep her safe—she couldn't trust anyone except herself. Maggie's experience highlights the fact that it is possible for someone to trust themselves yet be inherently mistrustful of others due to past experiences or personal beliefs. In Maggie's case, the trust she had in herself wasn't authentic. It came from a place of fear that she would be hurt, so she chose not to fully let anyone in. As Maggie experienced Heart Shift, she learned to trust herself and open up to others.

In contrast, Cheri's sense of self-trust came from a place of confidence and security within, which supported her ability to authentically trust others. She did not always have that inner confidence and security. She grew up in an alcoholic home and never knew which version of her father she was going to get—the one who was kind and loving or the one who was mean and spiteful. She lived in a state of high alert throughout much of her childhood.

Through our work together, Cheri learned about the disease of alcoholism and came to understand that her father's erratic behavior was a result of his disease and not anything she did or didn't do. By understanding this intellectually and then changing her subconscious belief through Heart Shift, Cheri realized she was not to blame. Growing up in such an environment heightened her natural intuitive abilities, which we all possess, enabling her to become an excellent judge of character. The issue for her was that she didn't trust her intuition. Heart Shift enabled her to not only listen but to trust and then act on her intuition.

When we have confidence in ourselves, we're inclined to take risks, knowing we can either overcome challenges or gain insights from them. Additionally, when we believe in our own judgment, it reinforces our decisions about others, including our choice to trust them. By having trust in our capability to cope with disappointments or betrayals, we become more open to taking chances with others because the possible adverse outcomes become less daunting.

When Cheri embraced her intuition by trusting and acting upon it, her experiences brought about positive outcomes, demonstrating the inherent value of self-trust. Similarly, Maggie cultivated trust in her own judgment, particularly in discerning whom to trust and when to open up to others. This not only enhanced her personal decision-making but also led to healthier, more meaningful relationships.

The reluctance to trust is rooted in fear. There are two types of fear:

1. Fear that keeps us safe
2. Fear that stops us from moving forward

The first type protects us from something dangerous. The second type stops us from doing something that is in our best interest. When you feel fear, identifying which type of fear you are experiencing is imperative.

Let's say you are an experienced hiker. You would most likely stay alert and watchful of your surroundings. If you hear the rustling of leaves or the snapping of twigs and branches as footsteps approach, an overwhelming sense of fear may come over you. I imagine you would stop and pay close attention. There could be a wild animal nearby, and if you ignore that fear, you could potentially put yourself in danger.

On the other hand, imagine you are embarking on a new career, maybe starting your own business. It's something you have always wanted to do, and there is so much excitement around it. Your website is designed, advertising is set up, customers are interested in your products or services, and you're about to sign the lease on office space. You feel intense fear. This may be the fear that comes from doing something new and different, even though you know opening your business is in your best interest.

When we turn within and allow ourselves to connect with fear, it often becomes clear what type of fear it is. By identifying the type of fear we are experiencing, we are able to discern whether to move forward or not. The ability to discern is what creates a sense of self-trust.

It's good to practice this with something that you are already certain is safe. If you like roller coasters, you might close your eyes and imagine yourself standing in line as the anticipation builds. Pay attention to all of your senses. Notice the fear that is there with the excitement. Where do you feel it in your body? Are you experiencing butterflies in your stomach? Is your heart pounding? What are the physical feelings that have presented themselves? What else do you notice? Allow these feelings to be your muscle memory for the kind of fear that is to be accepted, acknowledged, and pushed away. Do not allow them to be feelings that stop you.

Fear of the future is an offshoot of fear of moving forward. Those experiencing this type of fear often overthink and obsess about the future. While some degree of forward-thinking can be helpful, excessive thinking and worrying about the future is counterproductive. Knowing how to balance living in the now while preparing for the future is a critical component of living a joyous life. Meditation is a wonderful tool for managing this particular fear.

Silvia was so concerned about how she would support herself in retirement that she was not only afraid to spend money, but she also began hoarding. She didn't want to get rid of anything in case she "might need it one day." The kitchen reeked of old food delivery containers. Stacks of magazines and newspapers filled the dining room table. Her bedroom and spare room closets overflowed with clothes she hadn't worn in years. There were piles of cables, remote controls, old phones, and other outdated electronics. It had gotten so bad that her adult children stepped in and started clearing some things out of her house while she was at work. Although I didn't support the action they took, something needed to be done.

As we explored Silvia's fear, she shared that her mother, who was widowed at a young age, had a tough time financially as she got older. She had very little savings, and when she was diagnosed with dementia, it progressed rapidly. Due to her financial situation, she ended up in a facility that was less than desirable. The facility was old and run-down.

Her room was tiny, with very minimal natural light from one small window. The halls were dimly lit and emitted a musty odor. The staff was overworked, and while they took care of her basic needs, she rarely got a smile from any of them.

Silvia was committed to not having the same experience. Though, in reality, she had a fully funded pension, a paid-off home, and a long-term health care plan. The facts surrounding her financial situation didn't support her fear at all. In fact, her finances were in far better shape than many people her age.

As we further explored Silvia's fear through hypnosis, we uncovered a lengthy history of financial instability in her family. Not only did her mother have a challenging financial situation, but her grandparents also struggled in retirement, surviving on food stamps, Medicaid, and help from their children. Silvia had a belief that getting old means you have nothing—no money, no support. This belief was so strong that, even though her situation was different, she didn't see it that way. Silvia was afraid of moving forward, living fully, and trusting that she had planned for her future well. The subconscious beliefs she held about financial security, based on family history, were keeping her from the joyous, abundant life she had built for herself.

When someone is experiencing this degree of fear and anxiety, it is often necessary to start out slow and allow time for a shift to occur. In Silvia's case, due to the extreme pain she was in, she was committed to making a change.

Through regular and consistent meditation, visualization, and breathing techniques, Silvia felt an emotional shift. She didn't feel the same kind of panic and anxiety about the future and was able to be more rational. Her self-talk started changing. Now, she regularly thinks: "I've got a good plan. I'm confident."

Silvia is still a planner and is cautious with her spending; however, she is now able to trust in her financial situation and trust in herself to make prudent decisions. She has let go of things she no longer needs and is no longer afraid to spend money.

Ultimately, my goal is to support those I serve in learning to trust themselves. Within each of us are all the answers we need. It is a matter of learning how to tune in to that indwelling presence of life—or higher true self, as I like to call it—and listening to that voice. My role is to ask the questions that only you can answer for yourself.

I have recorded a meditation specifically designed for you to connect with your inner wisdom and identify what type of fear you are experiencing. Practice listening to this anytime you experience fear. The more you do, the easier it will be to identify the fear and release it. You will find the audio version of the meditation in the book portal. I invite you to listen to it often and allow it to support you in the practice of connecting and listening. The process is also written out here if you prefer to read through it.

Hypnosis to Identify Your Fear

Begin by focusing on your breath without trying to shift or alter it in any way—simply notice the inhale and the exhale. Allow yourself to lean into the rhythmic nature of the breath. Begin to notice a gentle wave of relaxation making its way down your body from head to toe, calming and relaxing you every step of the way. Feel that wave making its way down your head, the back of your head and neck, your facial muscles, and jaw, feeling calm and relaxed. As that wave continues down your throat and shoulders, allow them to drop just a bit. Now, the wave slowly continues down your arms all the way to your fingertips so they feel loose and limp—calm and relaxed.

As the wave makes its way down your chest and your back, both upper and lower, you feel deeply calm and relaxed. The wave continues down your abdomen, relaxing all of your abdominal muscles and organs. And now, the wave moves down your hips as you allow your body to sink even deeper into the surface you are sitting or lying on. Know that you are fully and deeply supported—deeply calm and relaxed. Now, the wave slowly makes its way down your legs all the way to your toes so that your entire body is now calm and relaxed, loose and limp.

From this place of deep relaxation, turn within to your inner wisdom, your intuition—the part of you that knows that it knows that it knows. Often, we feel this intuition in our gut, in the solar plexus. Imagine you are inhaling and exhaling from your solar plexus, activating the energy, wisdom, and guidance that lives there.

Bring to mind a time when you felt fear about something, and you did it anyway. You just knew it was the right decision, even though it scared you and you were right. Maybe it was something related to your education or work, or perhaps it was something involving a relationship. Moving through the fear paid off. Recall what it felt like when you decided to do whatever it was. Recall how your body felt—remember the emotions, thoughts, and physical sensations that came up at that time. Allow yourself to feel that.

Gently let that memory go and bring up a time when fear stopped you from doing something. Perhaps it involved being with a particular person, going somewhere, or taking on a business venture. Whatever it was, you sensed danger in some way and knew it was not for you. As you bring that up, remember how you felt—your body, your emotions, your thoughts. Take a few moments to really get in touch with what it felt like when you had a fear that was warranted.

Now, let it go. Clear your mind and bring up your current situation, opportunity, or whatever is causing you fear and perhaps stopping you from taking action. Allow yourself to feel the fear, and as you do, notice which type of fear it is. Is there danger? Is it honestly something unsafe for you? Or is it simply something new, different, or unfamiliar? Is it a fear of the unknown? Listen to your body, your heart, and your gut. Allow yourself to sense which type of fear it is.

You know the difference between danger or recklessness and the fear of a challenge or the unknown. Knowing what type of fear you are experiencing allows you to either move through it and proceed or stop moving forward and let it go.

Once you receive the clarity you've been looking for, allow gratitude to rise within you. Take a few deep breaths and bring yourself back to the present moment.

Hypnosis to Help Make a Choice

Begin by focusing on your breath without trying to shift or alter it in any way—simply notice the inhale and the exhale. Allow yourself to lean into the rhythmic nature of the breath. Now, notice a gentle wave of relaxation making its way down your body from head to toe, relaxing you every step of the way.

Feel that wave making its way down your head, the back of your neck, your facial muscles, and your jaw. You're beginning to feel calm and relaxed as that wave continues down your throat and shoulders, allowing them to drop just a bit. The wave slowly moves down your arms all the way to your fingertips, and they feel loose and limp—calm and relaxed. As that wave makes its way down your chest and your back, both upper and lower, you feel deeply calm and relaxed—very peaceful. The wave continues down your abdomen, relaxing all your abdominal muscles and organs, and then moves down your hips, allowing your body to sink even deeper into the surface you are sitting or lying on. You are deeply, deeply calm and relaxed—deeply supported. Now, feel that wave slowly making its way down your legs all the way to your toes so that your entire body is now deeply calm and relaxed, loose and limp.

Bring to mind a decision you're currently facing. Choose one of the options and visualize yourself having made that choice.

As you imagine that choice, allow yourself to feel it in your entire body, starting with your head. Imagine your intellect experiencing that choice. How might it impact your life or perhaps others? How does that choice affect the future and the present? Does it bring your energy level up or down when you think about making that choice?

Now, allow your energy to drop into your heart. Perhaps take a breath or two from your heart, fully connecting with your heart energy. How does making that choice feel in your heart? Is there a physical sensation, an emotion, or a thought that arises from your heart? Does your energy rise or diminish as you feel that decision from your heart?

Place your attention in your gut—your solar plexus. How does making that choice feel in your gut? Does it feel like the right thing to do? How does your energy feel—up or down? What does your gut say about this decision?

Let that go now. Release any energy that has come up around this decision. Take a few cleansing breaths as you let it go.

Now, visualize making the other choice. Let yourself completely accept that as your decision. As you do so, allow yourself to feel it, beginning with your head. Imagine your intellect experiencing that choice. How might it impact your life or perhaps others? How does that choice affect the future and the present? Does it bring your energy level up or down when you think about making that choice?

Allow your energy to drop into your heart. Perhaps take a breath or two from your heart, fully connecting with your heart energy. How does making that choice feel in your heart? Is there a physical sensation, an emotion, or a thought that arises from your heart? Does your energy rise or diminish as you think and feel that decision from your heart?

And now, place your attention on your gut—your solar plexus. How does making that choice feel in your gut? Does it feel like the right thing? How does your energy move? What does your gut say?

Know that connecting with your body in this way can shed much light on your choices. The more you connect with your body in this way, the clearer it becomes. Based on the feelings that rise up, you will sense what is the best choice for you.

Take three deep, cleansing breaths, and on the third exhale, open your eyes, shift around a bit in your seat, and feel yourself grounded and in the present moment.

Journal prompt

Reflect on the level of trust you hold within yourself.

- How does this inner trust influence your relationships with others?
- Explore the connection between your self-trust and your ability to extend trust to others.

Chapter 7

Visualization

"Visualization activates the same neural pathways in the brain that are activated when we actually do or experience the thing we are visualizing."

THE DAY CAROL first walked into my office, she plopped onto the couch, her jaw tight, and said, "I need hypnosis. I have a major surgery coming up, and I'm scared."

Although the surgery was not life-threatening, she had experienced complications in a prior procedure, and the fear was so great that simply going to the doctor for a pre-op visit created a full-blown panic attack. As she relayed the story to me, she shifted in her seat and nervously clasped her hands together.

"I felt my chest tighten, and I couldn't catch my breath. My heart was pounding so fast I thought I would have a heart attack." She stifled the tears as she said, "It was so bad I had to leave and reschedule. I don't know how I'm going to get through it." She broke down in tears.

Consciousness creates, and when we believe something, the subconscious mind works to prove it is true by drawing those experiences to us.

Carol understood this concept and believed it; however, she could not shift the belief and the emotion on her own. The realization that consciousness shapes reality brought even more fear for Carol. She felt she was creating potential complications. It was all snowballing in a painful way. Remembering that we can shift consciousness and place our attention on the positive is imperative. Consciousness doesn't manifest our thoughts instantly. If it did, things would be changing all the time due to our many varied thoughts and feelings. The key is to hone in on what the dominant thoughts are—those energized by the most emotion. Those are the ones most likely to manifest.

Neural pathways are the nerve fibers that carry information between the various parts of our central nervous system. They can form positive or negative associations and are extremely powerful in determining our emotions, actions, and behaviors. Consciousness arises from the intricate web of neural pathways and connections in our brains. These pathways, formed and reinforced through experiences and learning, dictate how we perceive and react to our outer environment.

Carol's memory of her previous surgery had created a neural pathway indicating surgery = complications. This created panic and fear every time she thought about her upcoming surgery. The good thing is that we have the ability to change these neural pathways through hypnosis, meditation, and visualization.

I had a similar experience, albeit on a smaller scale, with an in-office procedure on my sinuses. For the procedure, the doctor placed a heart rate monitor on my finger and reclined my chair. I recalled hearing the humming of the suction device and feeling the pressure in my sinuses. I remember that at that moment, I began to feel nervous and afraid. Suddenly, an alarm went off because my heart rate had skyrocketed. I knew at that moment I had a choice. I could remain panicked, and they might have to stop the procedure, or I could use the tools that I'd learned to calm myself. I chose to use my tools. I slowed my breath and took myself to what I like to call my happy place.

During hypnotherapy, I often guide my clients to go to their favorite, most relaxing place. This is a form of visualization. Having the sensation and the muscle memory of allowing your mind to take you there has the potential to create calm in just about any situation.

My personal happy place is by the ocean. I use all my senses to feel myself standing at the edge of the water. I feel the cool, wet sand between my toes, the cold water lapping over my feet, and the hot sun on my neck and back. I hear the waves coming in and out like breath. I smell the salty water in the air. I feel completely at peace.

Lying in that reclined chair at the doctor's office, I tapped into my senses to be there on that beach, and my heart rate started to go down. Calm and peace enveloped me as every muscle in my body began to loosen. The rest of the procedure went smoothly.

Another technique that can be helpful when someone is experiencing fear or anxiety is visualization of the future. For Carol, the visualization involved what would be possible once she had the procedure and went through recovery. Together, we created a scene of the activities that she would do, the places she would go, and the vacation that she was looking forward to. We played out the entire scene of her vacation using all her senses. We then created an anchor in the form of a hand position and a phrase to support her in recalling the vision when she needed it.

Carol saw herself on the island. Her eyes were greeted by a kaleidoscope of colors—the blue sky meeting the crystal-clear ocean at a distant horizon. She was surrounded by lush greenery, an array of vibrant flowers, and palm trees swaying gently in the breeze. The sunlight cast a warm, golden hue over everything. She could hear the rhythmic crash of waves against the shore.

Occasionally, the calls of birds created a melody that felt both new and nostalgic. The air was rich with the scent of saltwater mixed with the sweet fragrance of tropical flowers. The freshness of it, clean and invigorating, filled her lungs and cleansed her spirit with each breath. She could almost taste it—the blend of salt from the sea and a hint of floral sweetness. The warm sun kissed her skin, and the soles of her feet felt the softness of the sandy beach.

Carol's homework was to listen to the recording that I made for her every day. Doing this created a shift in her neural pathway and subconscious mind, which eliminated the panic attacks. Typically, you can begin to see a shift in a few weeks, but it can take up to a few months to see permanent change. Carol listened to the recording every day and played it as she was falling asleep. She was able to go through her surgery without panic and fear. I am happy to report that the surgery was a success!

The power of visualization is highlighted in a study conducted at the University of Chicago by Judd Biasiotto, a sports psychologist. Measuring basketball skills as the method, he randomly selected a group of students and tallied the percentage of free throws they made.

He then divided students into the following three groups:

- **Group 1:** Students practiced throwing free throws every day for one hour.
- **Group 2:** Students visualized themselves successfully throwing free throws every day for one hour.
- **Group 3:** Students did not practice, play basketball, or visualize.

The students were asked to come back after one month and take the same number of free throws as they initially did. The results were the following:

- **Group 1** improved by **24%**.
- **Group 2** improved by **23%**.
- **Group 3** had no change.

This is simply one of several studies that prove the power of visualization. When visualizing in a meditative state, we are activating the same neural pathways in the brain that are activated when we do or experience the thing we are visualizing. When we intentionally harness this power, the possibilities are unlimited.

One of the main components of Carol's success was her willingness to do her part. I almost always give my clients follow-up assignments to do at home. Sometimes it's journaling, sometimes it's visualization, sometimes it's meditation. Whatever it is, it's an integral part of supporting the work that we do in session and accomplishing the goal. I find that those clients who do the work at home have a much greater record of success.

Carol had a story based on her beliefs and fear of surgery. Her story was one of impending doom and helplessness. In rewriting her story, she tapped into the knowing that she had the power to shift her belief system and the knowing that the fear did not have to control her. She controlled the fear.

You will find a guided visualization in the book portal that takes you to your favorite, most relaxing place. I invite you to listen to the visualization often and allow it to create a neural pathway of peace that you can call upon whenever needed. The process is also written out for you.

Visualization: Favorite most relaxing place

Engaging in this practice several times can help you create a solid foundation for yourself.

Take a nice deep breath and then exhale completely. As you continue to breathe deeply, focus on slowly filling your lungs and belly, then emptying them completely. Allow the breath to support you in becoming calm and relaxed. Begin to recall your favorite, most relaxing place. It may be a place in your own home or a place outdoors. It should be someplace where you feel comfortable and relaxed.

Once you have this place in mind, use all of your senses to feel yourself there right now. Notice any aromas that are present. Perhaps it's the fresh air, ocean water, or a scented candle. Notice what you see in your favorite place. Are you gazing at the skyline or trees in nature? Or is it a painting on the wall of your home or vibrant colors around you? Feel what is around you. Perhaps there is a gentle breeze blowing through your hair, or your fingers are gently touching a flower petal. Maybe you can feel the texture of whatever you are sitting or standing on.

Now, tap into your sense of sound. Do you hear ocean waves, the wind rustling leaves, music, or laughter? What about your sense of taste? Can you taste the berries on the tree in front of you or the cool, refreshing drink you had last time you were at the beach? Allow all of your senses to be activated.

As your senses are heightened and you're fully present in your favorite, most relaxing spot, place the tip of your thumb and forefinger of your dominant hand together. Allow this to be an anchor for you. This anchor will support you in coming back to this memory when you use your senses to be in your favorite, most relaxing place. You can use this anytime you may be feeling stressed, fearful, or impatient. Allow yourself to install this anchor and know that you have the power to bring yourself right back here whenever you desire.

Take several minutes to sit in this feeling. When you feel complete, release your thumb and forefinger, take a deep cleansing breath, and open your eyes.

Journal prompt

- Have you ever had the experience of visualizing or imagining something, and it manifested?
- What is something you desire, and do you have a willingness to invest time in visualizing it?

Chapter 8

Affirmations

"The words we speak shape our reality."

SEVERAL YEARS AGO, I got that 2:00 a.m. phone call that no parent ever wants to get. My daughter had been in a serious car accident and was in the hospital.

My husband and I rushed to the hospital, but they wouldn't let us see her. An aide escorted us to a small room by ourselves to wait for whatever was to come next. As she approached the door, ready to leave us alone, I pleaded with her, "Is she all right? I need to see her!"

All she replied was, "You'll have to wait for the doctor." And then she shut the door behind her as she left.

As that door shut, the terror began to sink in. What could be so horrible that they wouldn't let us see her? My body began to tremble as the tears rolled down my cheeks. As the tears fell, something within me said, *No! Stop this thought pattern.*

Having experienced the power of affirmations and the spoken word, I immediately began speaking the affirmation: "She is whole, perfect, and complete. The healing currents of God are flowing through her body NOW."

I spoke it out loud to myself and even wrote it down on a scrap of paper I found in my purse. After several minutes, I began to feel my body relax. The shaking and tears had stopped, and I started to believe in my gut that all was well. It was as if a switch had been flipped. I noticed that my husband had stopped pacing and was now sitting beside me, holding my hand as we waited for the doctor.

After about 20 minutes—probably the longest 20 minutes of my life—the doctor came in and said we could see her. When we walked into the room, there were several doctors around her, one stitching her arm and another pulling pieces of glass out of her face as she lay there in a neck brace.

I felt completely helpless. All I wanted to do was take her in my arms and make the pain stop. My husband, normally stoic in this type of situation, was visibly shaken. His gaze moved from her to the doctors, as if looking for reassurance. I sensed that he, too, felt helpless.

We learned that she had a broken neck, a broken nose, multiple contusions, and—I don't know how many stitches. Fortunately, after spending a couple of days in the ICU, in addition to many weeks at home recuperating, she fully recovered.

As I look back on that time, the experience is almost surreal. After speaking the affirmation, it felt like something had taken over my body and my consciousness, enabling me to have the strength to believe all would be well.

An affirmation is a positive statement spoken in the present tense to shift your consciousness. Shifting our consciousness creates new neural pathways, which determine our emotions, actions, and behaviors. When one absolutely believes a positive outcome is possible and feels it strongly, it can be transformative.

While research is mixed on whether affirmations or affirmative prayer help others, there are studies showing that affirmations change the one speaking the affirmation. My personal belief is that we are all connected, and we are all one. If I change my consciousness, that goes into the field of oneness and can have a positive impact on others.

That day in the hospital, when I started speaking the affirmation, it wasn't just a source of solace for me; I noticed it also had a calming effect on my husband. My complete confidence in her full recovery wasn't simply my own belief—it became a beacon of hope for my husband and my daughter. They trusted in my faith, and that, in turn, bolstered their own faith and resilience.

We often pick up on the energy of those around us. If you find yourself in a group where people have a pessimistic view of their lives or current world events, you might notice a shift in your own feelings, tending toward negativity. Conversely, being in the company of those who maintain a positive and upbeat attitude can positively influence your own outlook on life.

As I stayed at my daughter's bedside throughout her hospital stay and continued to speak affirmations, I sensed she energetically connected with and embraced my confidence in her having a positive outcome. I witnessed her becoming stronger emotionally with each passing day. She was speaking more and showing interest in what was going on, even saying she couldn't wait to get home and see our dog.

In one study (Taber J.A. et al., 2016), survivors of cancer with an elevated sense of optimism experienced improved health, increased happiness, and more hope, along with a reduced incidence of cognitive decline. The conclusions drawn from these observations emphasize the potential for enhancing self-affirmation practices.

Several years ago, Gloria came to me for help. She had low self-esteem and was very critical and judgmental of herself. She also seemed to draw people into her life who criticized her and judged her. When I first met with her, she was very down, dejected, and didn't see any hope of shifting her circumstances.

"I never do anything right," she stated as she plopped down on the couch. "I always make bad decisions."

"Really?" I questioned. "You've never done anything right?"

"Well, that's what it feels like. There's no hope."

I assured her that although I was fairly certain she had done some things right, I believed her when she said it didn't feel that way. We started working with affirmations to allow her to begin to shift the behavior.

When working with affirmations, the goal is to stretch yourself a bit—but not so much that you don't believe what you are saying is possible. The feelings and emotions that arise when you speak your affirmation(s) matter. When we stretch too far, everything in us that says it's not possible overrides any words that we might say to the contrary.

If someone was struggling with money, and I told them to affirm, "I am a millionaire. I have all the money I could ever want or need," that would be so far from the truth that their consciousness would fight the statement, and it could actually make them feel worse.

Instead, I would craft the statement: "I am open (or willing) to experience abundance," or "I am willing to see all of my financial needs met."

These statements create a bridge and open the possibility of what is coming until the person is ready to affirm: "I experience abundance," or "I see all of my financial needs met."

As we discussed possible affirmations for Gloria, self-love and acceptance seemed to be the most useful qualities for her to affirm.

"How does 'I love myself completely' feel to you?" I asked her.

She scrunched up her eyes and shook her head. "I can't even say that."

"That's okay. Try this instead: 'I am willing to love and accept myself.'"

She sat back and took a deep breath. "I am willing to love and accept myself."

Noticing some hesitation but sensing she could stretch into it, I asked, "Does it feel like something you could start to believe?"

"Yes!" she exclaimed.

I asked Gloria to repeat the affirmation at least 50 times a day. I also instructed her to write it down every day and put up some Post-it notes where she'd see it. The next time I saw Gloria, there was a bit more sparkle in her eyes.

"I have noticed a shift in my self-talk," she said. "I'm not beating myself up in my head as much as I used to."

She shared that she had made a mistake at work—nothing huge, but still a mistake. "I couldn't believe how casual I was about it. I realized it, acknowledged it to my coworker, and fixed it." She added, "This is the kind of little thing that could've started a downward spiral."

This was a big step forward for Gloria, and the momentum it

provided supported her as we took a deep dive into her subconscious to access the source of her low self-esteem.

The practice of speaking affirmations and focusing on what was happening in the moment helped Gloria become present enough to create some excitement around the things she was doing. She was passionate about her work as a veterinary technician. She loved animals and provided comfort and loving care to them while they were receiving a vaccine or other medical treatments. This work gave her a sense of purpose and joy.

Another client, Vivian, came to me with a chronic medical condition that caused her a great deal of worry. She didn't know how the condition would progress or what limitations she might have in the future. The worry and obsession with the "what ifs" left her unable to fully appreciate the present.

One of the techniques I used with her was "right now" affirmations. My goal was to bring her to the present whenever she felt herself catastrophizing the future. The assignment was to notice when she was obsessing about the future, stop, and say out loud whatever she was seeing and doing. I instructed her to get very detailed in order to support the shift in focus.

For example, beyond simply saying, "Right now, I am taking a walk," she could say, "Right now, I am taking a walk and looking at the leaves on the trees. Right now, I am putting my right foot forward. Right now, I am watching a car drive by."

In his paper "The Science of Affirmations," Dr. David R. Hamilton describes how a University of Pennsylvania study showed that repeating self-affirmations produces physical changes in brain regions associated with self-processing, ultimately impacting people's perception of themselves. These changes are associated with subsequent positive changes in behavior.

Believing in the power of positive affirmations can set the stage for emotional resonance. This concept suggests that our emotional state influences our perceptions, behaviors, and interactions with others, which in turn shape the kinds of experiences and people we attract into our lives. When you are in a positive emotional state, you are more likely to perceive positive qualities in others and situations, thereby attracting more positive experiences and people.

Affirmations, like visualization, are directive practices. We use these practices when we are clear about what we desire to draw into our lives. As we affirm and visualize, we create new neural pathways that support the experiences we desire.

Dictionary.com defines affirmation as "the assertion that something exists or is true." The words we speak shape our reality. We speak what we believe to be true. This highlights why our self-talk is paramount. If I am constantly saying things like, "I'm so stupid. I never get anything right," or "I can't do this," or "I am never going to have the relationship I desire," then I am, in essence, calling these things into my life. By intentionally crafting positive affirmations, we can draw our desires to us.

As Vivian became more present by working on her "right now" affirmations, things started to change. She found a support group for people with chronic illnesses like hers and felt great solace in being with people who supported one another through the process. Her involvement in the group gave her purpose, and she found joy in embracing and supporting newcomers who were anxious about the future.

Key ingredients to a positive affirmation:

1. **Present tense:** Use phrases like "I am strong and confident" rather than "I will be strong and confident."
2. **First person:** Start your affirmation with "I" or "My" so the affirmation is personal to you.
3. **Positive phrasing:** Use affirmative words rather than negations. For example, say, "I am calm" instead of "I am not stressed."
4. **Concise:** Keep your affirmations simple and use words that resonate with you. A simple, clear statement is very powerful.
5. **Consider saying** "I am willing" or "I am open" when what you are affirming seems far from what you believe.

I invite you to start crafting some positive affirmations for yourself.

You might begin by thinking about an area of your life that you would like to improve. If it's greater self-love you desire, try, "I am (willing to be) kind and loving with myself." For more guidance or direction, you might affirm, "I am guided every step of the way on my journey."

The more feeling and emotion we put into our affirmations, the more power they have. Allow yourself to be excited and energized by your affirmations. You will find more sample affirmations in the book portal to assist you in creating your own.

Journal prompt

- Think about something you desire to shift and write a couple of affirmations. Be sure to review the key ingredients to a positive affirmation in this chapter. You might also refer to the examples in the book portal to help get you started.
- Notice what happens after spending some time repeating the affirmations. Does it feel more possible? Has there been a shift? Do you feel different?

Chapter 9

Self-Love

"Prioritizing your well-being above others is a necessary component of cultivating self-love."

EMBRACING SELF-LOVE IS essential to living a happy and fulfilled life. It goes beyond massages and spa treatments. Don't get me wrong—there is nothing wrong with that type of self-care. True self-love dives deeper to include holding yourself in high regard and honoring your time and energy. It grows from consciously taking actions that support your physical, spiritual, and emotional needs. Prioritizing your well-being above others is a necessary component of cultivating self-love. There are three main aspects of self-love:

- Saying no and prioritizing yourself.
- Finding balance and honoring your desires.
- Gratitude and loving-kindness toward yourself.

#1: Saying No and Prioritizing Yourself

As a recovering people-pleaser, I know all too well the toll it can take when we consistently put others' needs ahead of our own. When my kids were little, I worked part-time from home, ran the financial end of the business my husband and I owned, took care of everything around the house, and cooked a family meal almost every night. Since I was fortunate enough to be a "stay-at-home" mom, I also always said yes to requests to volunteer at my kids' school and our spiritual center. What I failed to realize was that I was basically working two full-time jobs!

On a typical day, I'd wake the kids and get them off to school, then come home and dive into our family business for several hours. This was followed by tasks from my part-time job. Then, in what felt like a blink, it was time to pick up the kids. We'd often stop at the grocery store or do other errands after school, even though the kids were usually not up for it after a long day. Once home, I'd prepare a family dinner to enjoy together. Afterward, it was the kids' bedtime routine, followed by catching up on volunteer work, laundry, and other chores. Personal time was nonexistent. My moments with the kids often felt hurried, and my mind was frequently elsewhere, preoccupied with the next task.

I chose to work only part-time once I had kids because my journey to becoming a mother was long and challenging, so I wanted to spend as much time as possible with them. One night, as I lay in bed, my mind reeling about what was on the agenda for tomorrow, I realized that my people-pleasing and inability to say no were defeating the purpose of my choice. I wasn't spending as much time with them as I wanted, and the time I did spend with them lacked the meaningful connection I longed for. I found myself squeezing in the creative projects they loved, trying to keep them occupied so I could get a little more work done rather than sitting with them and enjoying our time together. I felt like I wasn't giving enough to them or to my work. And there was nothing left for me. It was time for me to make a shift.

One of my mentors helped me tremendously when he said, "When you say no, you have the opportunity to say yes to something else, and someone else has the opportunity to step up and say yes."

It was so simple and so true. As I started practicing using my voice and saying "no," it was empowering and not always easy. I actually had an opportunity to say no to my mentor. He asked if I would be willing to be on the board at the spiritual center, and I initially said I would think about it. I knew that I didn't have the time for what that role would entail, and I couldn't imagine saying no to him! Even the thought made me feel guilty.

Then I remembered his words, picked up the phone, took a deep breath, and said no.

He casually said, "It's fine. No is a perfectly good answer."

I breathed a sigh of relief, and from that moment on saying no began to get easier.

In taking this step and saying no that first time, I started to understand how saying no led to prioritizing myself. By saying no to some of the activities I had been doing, I found more time to be fully present with my kids, which shifted my self-talk around what kind of mother I was. I went from saying things in my head like, "I'm not spending enough time with them. What if they don't feel all the love I have for them?" and "Am I messing them up?" to "I feel so connected to my children, and I know they feel it too."

I have had many clients struggle with saying no and sincerely honoring their desires. Many of us have been taught that others' needs carry more weight than our own. When we go against that learned behavior, we can feel selfish. The truth is that loving yourself and honoring your needs and desires allows you to be more available for what really matters. It's like the flight attendants tell you, "Please secure your own mask before assisting others." If you don't take care of yourself, you can't take care of others either.

When I first met Sarah, she complained of exhaustion.

"I don't know how much longer I can go on like this. I am not even enjoying the things I normally love," she said, fighting back tears.

"What's got you so tired all the time?" I asked.

"Work and the animals. They need me, and I can't say no. They're helpless," she sniffled through her tears.

Her days were jam-packed from morning till night. She had a full-time job and filled her evenings and weekends with volunteer activities. She had a big heart, and much of her volunteer work was at a local animal shelter where she also organized fundraisers. She loved animals; it was a passion of hers. Every time something else was needed—an extra shift at the shelter, making calls, or planning the next fundraiser—they turned to Sarah because she always said yes.

The busyness, lack of sleep, and lack of time for a social life were taking a toll on Sarah's health. She had become increasingly irritable and short-tempered, snapping at trivial annoyances, such as someone in front of her not holding the door open, and fuming over small inconveniences like traffic. She didn't have time to prepare healthy meals, which had always been a priority to her. Instead she was stopping at the Wendy's drive-through after work every day, feeling sluggish from the lack of healthy eating. She desperately wanted to make a change but didn't know where to begin.

Through hypnotherapy, we came to understand the source of Sarah's apparent inability to say no. She lacked the nurturing that she desired as a child, and the way she got love and had her emotional needs met was by doing things for her parents. At the young age of seven, she was not only participating in the upkeep of the home—vacuuming and dusting—but was responsible for things she was far too young to be responsible for. Sarah often cooked the family meal when using the stove, and sharp knives were not safe. She was also responsible for her younger siblings, one of whom was only three and needed close supervision. She prepared their meals, fed and bathed the three-year-old, and did laundry.

Sarah believed, *"I am not lovable. If I am helpful, they will need me and love me."*

Sarah had two cats and a dog in the home growing up. Her love for these animals and the love they gave her in return sparked her passion for helping the animals in the shelter. Sarah's favorite childhood memories were those spent with her pets. She was able to escape the responsibilities at home by taking the dog on long walks through the forest and by the lake. At the end of the day, curling up in bed with the cats and dog and feeling their heartbeats against her chest gave her the feeling of being loved.

As we worked together, I shared my three-step plan to honor time and energy.

1. **PAUSE.** Take a breath. Allow yourself a moment to be present and notice how you feel when asked to do something—whether it is being of service in some way, an activity, or a social gathering. Give yourself a moment to center yourself.

2. **INQUIRE.** Ask yourself how it would feel to say yes, and then ask yourself how it would feel to say no. Notice how your body physically feels with each question. Do you feel tension and heaviness, or does your energy rise? Our body is always informing us. Remember, if you struggle with saying no, a response such as, "Let me think about it," or "I will let you know later," is perfectly acceptable. Once you've had the opportunity to connect with yourself, undistracted by the pressure to respond quickly, your response will be more authentic.

3. **RESPOND.** Whether your answer is "yes," "no," or "I will let you know," the key is that you are authentic and respond from a place of self-love. The joy in seeing someone's pleasure in your *yes* will fade quickly if you don't feel joy in the *yes.*

As Sarah integrated these steps, time started opening up for her. She began saying no to the things that had been draining her energy, such as extra shifts at the shelter. While she loved the animals, she realized that overextending her time left her feeling resentful. At first, the shelter manager pushed back; however, when Sarah clearly set the boundary of how much time she would spend there, the manager accepted it. The time Sarah spent there was much more enjoyable, and she had time for other activities. She engaged in cooking, which had been a passion of hers. She also rekindled some friendships that were meaningful to her.

#2: Balance and Honoring Your Desires

Self-love is not only about saying no. It is about being authentic and nurturing yourself.

I am fortunate to have the ability to create my own schedule. Recently, I realized that I wasn't creating the schedule and balance that I desired. I loved all the things I had said yes to and was participating in; however, my schedule was so full that I lacked free time for spontaneous activities. There was no room for a last-minute lunch with my husband or a long walk on a beautiful day.

As I turned within and got curious, I realized a small wave of lack was creeping up in my consciousness. I was afraid that if I limited my availability to see clients, they wouldn't be able to schedule, and it would impact my financial security. In my studies as a spiritual practitioner, we would call this "second crop." It means that some limiting belief you have worked through and let go of is starting to sneak up on you again.

In taking time to reflect and meditate, I was able to recognize the fear for what it was and not allow it to run wild. When I finally streamlined my availability, clients were still easily able to schedule.

I have now once again created the space and time in my schedule to be spontaneous and feel freedom. If it is a particularly beautiful day, I have time to take a walk, feeling refreshed and invigorated as I move my body. If I get a last-minute invitation I would like to accept, I can say yes.

This is why it is imperative to have practices, resources, and people in your life who support you in having dominion over your life. While we all have certain obligations and bills to pay, within those parameters, we still have the choice to prioritize ourselves.

#3: Gratitude and Loving-Kindness Toward Yourself

One of the biggest choices we have is our attitude. An attitude of gratitude can go a long way toward infusing more joy and love into your life.

Dr. Robert A. Emmons of the University of California and Dr. Michael E. McCullough of the University of Miami conducted a study on gratitude. Participants were asked to write a few sentences each week focusing on the following topics:

- Group one wrote about things they were grateful for that had happened during the week.

- Group two wrote about daily irritations or things that had upset them.
- Group three wrote about events that had affected them without an emphasis on positive or negative aspects.

After ten weeks, those who wrote about gratitude were more optimistic and felt better about their lives. Surprisingly, they also exercised more and had fewer visits to physicians than those who focused on sources of aggravation.

How can we apply this to our lives? There are several simple steps you can take to begin expressing more gratitude. Here are a few examples:

- Write five things you are grateful for about yourself each evening.
- Tell at least one person every day what you appreciate about them.
- Make a gratitude jar and add a note about something you are grateful for daily.
- Commit to at least one random act of kindness each day.
- Write down three things you are grateful that you get to do each morning.
- At dinner with loved ones, invite each person to share something they are grateful for.

Experiment with these and see what feels good for you. The more we practice anything, the easier and more natural it becomes. Allow gratitude to become a new habit. When we focus on what we are grateful for, it can lead to greater contentment and appreciation for the lives we are living. Being grateful for our accomplishments and ways of being builds self-love and appreciation.

I committed to at least one random act of kindness daily a while back. I made it a point to hold doors open, let someone go ahead of me in a line, and give a compliment to someone. It lifted my mood and brought me so much joy. During that time, someone paid for my Starbucks order in the drive-through, and someone else paid my toll!

When Ashley came to me, she was struggling with a particular friendship.

"Cindy is always asking me to do something for her," Ashley complained. "She goes out of town for work so much, and I have to watch her cats. She also borrows my car a lot."

"Tell me how the friendship serves you," I asked.

"Well," she hesitated slightly, "Cindy is a great listener, and she is definitely my go-to when there's something I need to talk through." Her tone of voice became softer, and she smiled. "She also always tells me the truth. Whether it's my new outfit or red flags with a boyfriend, Cindy always tells it like it is. She's really the only one of my friends I can trust to be honest in that way."

The friendship actually felt solid and balanced, with both women giving and receiving.

It turned out that Ashley's struggle was related to previous relationships where she was taken advantage of. By recognizing what she gained from the friendship and feeling gratitude for it, the trigger of the past dissolved.

Ultimately, saying no, creating balance, and practicing gratitude can all play vital roles in experiencing more self-love. Saying no to things that drain our energy, compromise our values, or hinder our personal growth creates space for what really matters. It is an act of self-care—a gentle reminder that our well-being matters. Balance is the sweet spot where our physical, emotional, and spiritual selves come into harmony. It's a delicate dance that requires attention and care to bring peace and allow your true essence to shine. By cultivating gratitude, we shift our focus from what's lacking to what's present. The things we focus on tend to increase.

As you reflect on the aspects of self-love I mentioned, I invite you to consider what resonates with you. Is there a particular area that could use more of your focus? In the book portal, I have several recorded meditations on self-love that can help you get in touch with where you might be lacking self-love and how to increase it. You're invited to follow along here in the book or listen to the audio version on the book portal—whichever feels most supportive of you in this moment.

Self-love

Sit or lie down comfortably with your body supported and gently close your eyes. Focus your attention on your breath, noticing the coolness of the air right where it enters your nostrils. Gently breathe in for the count of three, hold for one second, and then exhale for the count of three. Do this three times, allowing your body and mind to relax.

Visualize a beautiful tree at the beginning of fall. This tree is tall and has lots of branches. Imagine that you are one of the leaves on the topmost branch, and very slowly, picture yourself floating down toward the earth on a gentle breeze. Feel yourself becoming more relaxed as you float lower and lower until you gently land on the soft grass, feeling and relaxed, supported, and warm.

As you lie there in the soft grass, allow yourself to feel the nurturing that comes from Mother Earth. Sense yourself as one with all of nature, knowing that everything you need comes to you when you need it. Notice how the gentle rhythm of your heart beats in time with all of nature, knowing you are always loved and supported. Now, visualize a golden glow within your heart and see it glowing and flowing throughout your entire body, cleansing and healing you of all your hurt and distress, and soothing every bit of pain and anger. It is replaced with unconditional love from your own heart. Declare to yourself right now: I love and accept myself exactly as I am. I deserve love, and I accept love now. I attract loving, healthy relationships into my life. All my relationships are healthy, whole, and healed as I experience an abundance of love in my life.

Feel the wondrous sense of belonging that comes from being a part of all that is around you. Allow the love flowing through your heart and body to now be extended to those around you. This is a reciprocal universe, and what you give out returns to you multiplied. There is always enough love—more than enough love.

When you are ready, bring your attention back to the room and take a few deep breaths as you open your eyes. Know that you are loved, and all is well in your world.

Love All of Yourself!

Allow yourself to get into a comfortable position, with your arms and legs uncrossed, your back supported, and turn your focus to your breath. Take a nice deep breath to the count of five, hold for a moment, and exhale to the count of five. Repeat this breath pattern two more times. Allow your body to relax and feel fully supported by the surface you are sitting or lying on.

Bring to mind an image of yourself as a child at whatever age may rise up in you. Simply allow the image of yourself as a child to form. Look at that child and tell them that you love them. Tell them that they are here to do wonderful, joyful things and that you are going to be their biggest cheerleader. Look deeply into their eyes. Notice what you see. If there are any worries, fears, or sadness, reassure them that this will pass. Imagine opening your heart and sending loving energy to your child self. You might imagine that you're taking this child by the hand or holding them in your arms—whatever feels comfortable. Provide the comfort that your child self needs. Remain in this energy for as long as you feel called to. When it feels complete, visualize your child self running off joyfully, playing and doing whatever it is that they love to do. As that image fades away, take a nice cleansing breath.

Now, bring up another image of yourself a little older, perhaps in your teen years or as a young adult. As you bring this image of yourself up in your mind and see them standing before you, speak words of affirmation: I love you. You're beautiful inside and out. You're here to live a joyful, happy, fulfilling life. I am here to support you.

Notice how your younger self responds to these words. Look into their eyes and notice what emotions they are experiencing. Reassure them that all is well, that everything is falling into place exactly as it is meant to be. Reassure them that you love them and visualize yourself pouring love upon that part of yourself. See your younger self accepting and receiving all of that beautiful, loving energy. See the loving energy strengthening them, supporting them, and building confidence within them. Spend some time with that part of yourself, continuing to pour love upon them. As you feel complete with this part of yourself, simply see them fading off, doing what brings them joy, happiness, and purpose.

And now, imagine filling yourself with beautiful, loving energy right here, right now, right where you are. Allow the loving energy to fill you to overflowing. What is it you need to hear? What is it that you would like to experience to feel love and appreciation? What is the path to giving that love to yourself? Is it allowing yourself to have more rest to take care of your physical body? Is it how you move your body? Perhaps it's saying no to the things that really aren't yours to do—the things that don't light you up. Maybe it's saying yes to something that you've wanted to do but, for whatever reason, didn't pursue. What is yours to do right now? Is it to love and honor yourself, your dreams, and your desires? Take time to listen to your intuition, to that inner voice. Feel it and know that through love, anything is possible. Allow yourself to be in the stillness and listen.

When you are ready to bring your attention back to the room, take three deep, cleansing breaths, and on the third one, exhale. Open your eyes, shift around a little bit in your seat, and feel yourself completely present and completely awake in the now.

Listen to Your Body Hypnosis

Get in a comfortable position, ensuring your arms and legs are uncrossed, and begin to place your attention on your breath without any effort to shift or alter it in any way. Notice the inhale and notice the exhale. Allow yourself to become aware of the rhythmic nature of the breath—the reciprocity of the breath. Now, begin to notice on the exhale a wave of relaxation making its way down your body from head to toe, calming and relaxing you every step of the way. Feel that wave making its way down your head, down the back of your head and neck, relaxing your facial muscles and jaw. Feeling calm and relaxed as that wave continues down your throat and shoulders, allowing your shoulders to drop just a bit. Feel the wave making its way slowly down your arms, traveling all the way to your fingertips so that they're loose and limp. You're beginning to feel deeply calm and relaxed.

As the wave moves down your chest and back—both upper and lower—you become more and more calm and relaxed as the wave makes its way down to your abdomen, relaxing all of your abdominal muscles and organs. Allow your body to sink even deeper into the surface you are sitting or lying on, feeling fully and deeply relaxed. Feel the wave continue down your hips, slowly moving down your legs all the way to your toes. Your entire body is now deeply calm and relaxed, loose and limp.

In a few moments, I'm going to invite you to do a gentle scan of your body. As you're scanning your body, I want you to notice where you feel any sense of pain or discomfort—or perhaps simply a sense that something is there wanting to be explored. When you notice something, pause and place all of your energy upon that part of your body. Imagine sending loving energy from your heart to that part of your body. Energetically express appreciation and love for all that it does for you. Once you feel a strong connection and a deep appreciation for that part of your body, energetically inquire what it is trying to tell you. What does it need you to know right now? Listen carefully.

Allow yourself to be wildly curious about what your body is trying to tell you. Ask energetically whatever questions arise based on what you're sensing and feeling and what that body part tells you. Be curious about what you can do to support that part of your body. Once you feel that you have received all the information available for you at this moment, express appreciation and gratitude for this information. If you sense that there is something you need to do in order to support your body, you might commit to doing it at this time. Let your body know that you will provide what it is asking for.

Once you have received the information and expressed gratitude, you may either move on and continue the scan of your body, repeating the curiosity and appreciation, or you may have attended to the one area that needed support from you at this time. You may also notice other areas that require attention.

When you are complete with your body scan, take three slow, deep, cleansing breaths, and on the third breath, open your eyes, shift around in your seat, and allow yourself to become fully present and in the now.

Journal prompt

- As you consider the three aspects of self-love, to what degree do you practice each of them?
- What could you do to embrace self-love even more?

PART III

Chapter 10

Heart Shift Using Affirmations, Meditation, and Visualization

Mary's Story

WHEN MARY WALKED into my office, her steps were slow and hesitant. As she sat on the couch, she slumped down as if carrying a heavy weight.

"I feel emotionally shut down with my fiancé, and I don't know why," she said. "It feels like I can't trust him."

"Tell me what he's like," I inquired.

"He's very social and extroverted. He does drink a lot," she said, gazing down at the floor. "I'm not interested in drinking and don't enjoy it when I occasionally do have a drink."

In exploring her early childhood, she shared that her parents divorced when she was young. Her mom shared things with her at that time that were not appropriate for their relationship. Her mother was depressed and an alcoholic. Her dad remarried, and Mary did not have a good relationship with her stepmother. She blamed her stepmother for her parents' divorce, although her parents divorced long before the stepmother came into the picture.

During our first session, we did a simple process so that I could see how responsive she was to hypnosis.

I performed an induction to bring her into a trance state. "Allow your attention to be placed upon your heart energy," I instructed her. "Imagine yourself in a place where your heart feels content and you are tuned into all the loving energy in your heart."

"I'm at the beach, and the sun is pouring down on me," she said with a huge smile on her face.

"Tell me more about how it feels."

"I feel a gentle breeze on my face, and I'm dipping my toes into the water."

"Now, use all of your senses to feel yourself right there on the beach," I said.

The look of contentment that appeared on Mary's face was all I needed to see to know that she was very responsive. The bonus to her was that spending time in a relaxed and peaceful state provided comfort to her.

For hypnotherapy, or actually any therapy, to be productive, there must be a sense of trust and rapport between the therapist and client. This is why I like to start slow and fully evaluate where the client currently is in order to tailor my Heart Shift method to the client's needs and desires.

When Mary arrived for our next session, she was quite upset and agitated. Her brows were furrowed, and her lips were turned down. As she sat in my office with her arms crossed, her foot was rapidly tapping on the floor. She told me that the day before, while she was using her fiancé's phone to check the weather, she accidentally stumbled upon a text message from a woman named Emily. The message read, "Had a great time last night. Can't wait to see you again."

Mary's heart sank. She said that she felt like she had been punched in the gut. She couldn't believe that he would cheat on her. In previous relationships, infidelity had been an issue. Her fiancé, however, had never given her a reason to mistrust him. She did not say anything to him at the time and was quite torn as to what to do. When she thought about the possibility of him cheating on her, she hesitated to confront him because she knew it would be the end of the relationship.

We all have the ability to tune in to our higher self—that part of us that is our most intuitive self—and get the guidance we need. While she was in trance, I guided Mary to get in touch with her inner intuitive voice.

"I can't just let this go. It's eating me up inside," she said.

"And what exactly is your inner voice telling you to do?"

"Stay calm and ask him about the text," she calmly stated.

I then told her to visualize herself getting ready to speak to him. I told her to see herself calm, grounded, and confident, trusting that he would be honest, no matter what that would entail.

"I know I can do this. I must know the truth. I deserve to know the truth," she said confidently.

When we are in a hypnotic trance, we access our subconscious mind. This is where we truly create our experience of life. By getting in touch with her higher self and knowing that she wanted honesty and trustworthiness in her partner, Mary's only option was to have a conversation. She was very much in touch with the fact that she was worthy of the honesty and faithfulness she desired, which gave her the confidence she needed.

At our next session, Mary shared that when she spoke to her fiancé, he explained that Emily was actually an old college friend who was in town for a few days. He had met up with her for dinner the night before to catch up, but nothing had happened between them. He showed Mary the rest of the text messages between him and Emily, which were completely innocent. Mary was grateful that she took the time to gather herself and confront him in a calm manner. She felt a sense of confidence in herself and was very relieved by the outcome.

After this instance, Mary confided to me that she was still concerned about her hesitation to fully open up with her fiancé.

"I feel so much better when I just say what's on my mind. Why do I hesitate so much?" she asked. "I even hesitate with friends sometimes."

Our next session focused on the source of Mary's hesitation to open up. As I guided her while in hypnosis to the source of the hesitation, she went to the time in her life when her parents were going through their divorce.

When we go back in time, we often return to childhood. However, it is not to blame or shame our caregivers. It is to uncover what the child came to believe. The beliefs that we adopt about ourselves and life at a young age stay with us in the subconscious mind. These beliefs then write the story of our lives. When we access the source of these beliefs with the consciousness of an adult, we can dismantle them and rewrite our story.

Mary was six years old at the time of the divorce, and at that age, children generally see their world as revolving around them. When her father left, she believed it was her fault—as if there was something inherently wrong with her and her father must have seen it and left because of it. Of course, that wasn't at all true. In believing this about herself, she became shy, quiet, and reserved. She subconsciously believed that if others saw this "truth" about her, they would leave too. She was afraid to speak up and be herself.

In order to clearly see this pattern in her life and how it impacted her, I guided her forward while in hypnosis; she went to a memory of when she was a little bit older at school and she made a mistake on an assignment. This is what happened:

Teacher: "Class, you must pay close attention to the instructions. Look at what Mary did."

She then proceeded to point out the details of Mary's mistake. While Mary had gotten most of the answers on her math correct, she failed to show her work as instructed.

Mary thought: *I am so stupid. Everyone is looking at me. I want to crawl into my desk. I never want to come back.*

Mary believed: *Now everyone knows I'm stupid. I have to keep to myself.*

After this event, Mary withdrew and shared even less of herself.

As we progressed further in hypnosis, she went to a time when she was a little older. Her mom was getting ready to go out for the evening as she did most nights. She typically left right after dinner and came home drunk in the early hours of the morning. This left Mary home alone most evenings, terrified that something bad would happen to her mother and she'd never make it home. Mary would stay up into the night waiting to hear her mother stumble through the door, relieved that she made it home. She told herself that she didn't need anyone and was just fine by herself. In truth, she was lonely and sad. She felt her mother didn't think she was worth staying home for.

To shift the beliefs and conclusions she had formed due to the experiences in her life, we touched back on the six-year-old she was when the behavior of being withdrawn and shy first began. Mary was able to bring up an image of herself at that age, look into that little girl's eyes, and energetically communicate with that part of herself. She was able to see her adult self holding that child, comforting her, and asking her what she needed to feel safe enough to open up and trust people. Great clarity came through. That child needed positive self-talk, without judgment.

This was the first big step in the healing process. Knowing what is needed is essential. Knowing how to give ourselves what is needed is equally vital. This is where spiritual practices come in to support us. In Mary's case, positive affirmation was the tool that we used.

As I explained in the chapter on affirmations, over time, with consistent repetition, positive affirmations can help reshape an individual's self-image and belief system, leading to greater self-acceptance, self-love, and a more positive outlook on life. These are particularly powerful when used in meditation and hypnosis.

Mary began to talk to her child self in a loving and compassionate way. She expressed love and assured her younger self that the issues between her parents had nothing to do with her. She reassured her that she had done nothing wrong and that she was perfect just as she was. Mary let her younger self know that she was free to be a little girl who laughed, played, and enjoyed all the things she loved. By communicating with her child self in this way, that part of her subconscious—the source of the false beliefs—began to shift. Some of the affirmations that Mary used were: "I am enough," "I am worthy of love and happiness," and "I fully love and accept myself."

Over the next several weeks, Mary repeated these affirmations and used them as a mantra during her meditation time. As a result, she started to observe a transformation in her behavior. She shared more of herself with her fiancé and engaged in meaningful conversations about her desires and vision for their future together.

"I've told my fiancé that I don't like it when he drinks a lot, and for the first time, I was able to tell him why," she said. "It felt scary to tell him how much my mom's drinking impacted me, but once I got it out, it felt like something that was standing between us had been removed."

Although the conversations weren't always easy, Mary felt the words flowing far more comfortably than ever before. "It's like I have this inner strength that grows every time I stretch and share more deeply," she told me.

As she became more confident in her personal relationship, Mary wanted to discuss her professional path. She was a successful account executive for an advertising agency. She felt that she had lost her passion for the work; however, the security of a steady income was essential to her. She increasingly found herself immersed in a sense of dread at the mere thought of going to work each morning and spent her afternoons intently watching the clock, eagerly anticipating the moment when the workday would finally end.

As Mary turned within during hypnotherapy, she realized that she actually still had a passion for the work she was doing. We made a list of the parts she enjoyed:

- She excelled at building relationships and understanding people's needs and goals, which served her well in her role as a liaison between the client and the agency.
- She enjoyed collaborating with other members of the agency's team and had a good rapport with the creative directors, copywriters, and others on the team.
- She excelled at identifying new business opportunities and developing proposals to pitch to prospective clients.

The part of her work she did not enjoy or feel confident doing was negotiating pricing, budgets, and other contract details. She realized she had been so focused on the hard parts that weren't her natural strengths that she didn't allow herself to spend time cultivating those strengths—people skills and relationship building—and being more present to them.

All of us possess certain innate abilities—talents that come effortlessly to us. As we cultivate those skills, we step into our realm of brilliance, where we can shine. While we can develop and improve our skills in other areas, pursuing something that doesn't come naturally to us can only take us so far.

If you have a passion for singing but struggle to stay on pitch, you may be able to improve with a vocal coach and diligent practice. However, you might still find it challenging to establish a singing career. Not all of us can be Alicia Keys. Someone who possesses a natural affinity for singing and loves it can hone their skills and genuinely excel.

After that session, Mary's assignment was to practice tuning in to her higher self. She did this during her regular meditation time by imagining that she was breathing into her gut and activating the energy of her intuitive self. She would ask herself things like, "What is mine to do today?" or "How can I use my gifts and talents to serve the agency, my clients, and myself?" The more she tuned in and practiced, the more guided she felt.

Mary devised a plan based on the insights uncovered during the hypnotherapy session and subsequent meditations. She decided to prioritize relationship-building and communication—her natural strengths—and delegate budget and pricing tasks to her staff. Although she still had oversight of the budget, she didn't dedicate much of her working time to it. Instead, she familiarized herself with it, passed off the daily tasks to her staff, and directed her focus to what she did best. The result was that she was more productive, and her passion for the work returned. Now, as she arrived at work, she was uplifted at the thought of who she would be connecting with that day.

Mary continues to meditate and hone her ability to connect with her higher self. The benefits of this practice have extended to other aspects of her life, including her wedding planning. Mary has utilized her strengths in planning and organization while allowing her fiancé to contribute in a way that makes him feel confident and accomplished. He loves balancing the budget and attending to scheduling details. As a result, they have created a harmonious experience while navigating the complexities of a large wedding with extended family.

My goal when working with clients is to empower them. By equipping Mary with the necessary tools to listen to her inner voice and trust her instincts, she acquired valuable skills that will benefit her in the long run. During hypnotherapy sessions, she experienced breakthroughs and "aha" moments. However, the impact of these moments really took off when she put in the effort and practiced outside of the sessions.

Mary demonstrated a willingness and openness to do her part, which allowed her to effectively and joyfully make changes and demonstrate a Heart Shift. She went from being shut down and mistrustful to trusting her intuition and confidently taking charge of her career and personal life. The use of meditation, visualization, and affirmations supported her Heart Shift.

Journal prompt

- Do you see yourself in Mary's difficulty in opening up and trusting?
- If so, how does it show up?
- Are you clear about your strengths, and does your life reflect that clarity?

Chapter 11

Heart Shift Using Self-Love

Valerie's Story

"I JUST DON'T KNOW what to do anymore. When I met David, he told me he was divorced. But that wasn't true," Valerie said as she fidgeted with her hands.

"And how did it feel when you found out?" I asked, leaning forward.

"I feel betrayed and confused. I love him. He's kind and loving in so many ways," she sobbed into her hands. "I feel cared for and loved when I'm with him. I thought I could get past it, but those initial lies…they're always in the back of my mind. I can't trust him."

By the time Valerie found out about David's marriage, she was already committed to the relationship and wanted to make it work. The lack of trust was making it more and more difficult as time went on.

Valerie is a very bright, successful clothing designer, and her clothes are in several major retail stores. Her confidence and self-assurance shine in the way she runs her business, which operates smoothly like clockwork. She handles interactions with her staff and manufacturers with mastery. The thought of doubting her ability to support herself and maintain independence has never crossed her mind.

There was a great contrast between the way Valerie ran her business and the way she was in intimate relationships. She did not understand why there was such a difference, and she had a great desire to have a partner and a family. The relationships that she had been in up to this point were not what she considered marriage material.

Valerie's previous partner lacked the drive to achieve financial success. He frequently switched jobs without making significant progress in his career or fully committing to any particular job. He was a CPA but hadn't stayed at any firm for longer than a year and took months off in between jobs. As Valerie was accomplished in her own career and financially secure, she desired a partner who shared the same values. It was evident that this man did not prioritize financial success in the same way.

Another man Valerie dated struggled with commitment. His previous relationships demonstrated his difficulty in maintaining long-term connections, as he had never been with one person for more than six months. Whenever Valerie brought up the subject of marriage or their future together, he would evade and redirect the conversation. It was clear that he did not hold commitment and relationships in the same high regard as Valerie did.

Both men showed their true selves early on, yet Valerie overlooked these warning signs and continued the relationships. When both relationships eventually ended, Valerie felt hurt and disappointed.

I was curious as to why an accomplished, intelligent, and successful woman would choose partners who clearly did not share her values. I was also curious about her current relationship and what might have been evident early on that she wasn't consciously aware of at this point.

Although Valerie continued her relationship with David after finding out he was married and living with his wife, she did not fully open up to him. She simply didn't trust him with her heart. David appeared different from her previous relationships, and I sensed that was what kept her involved with him. He was very successful and loved talking about the future, including plans to divorce his wife and marry her. He told Valerie everything she wanted to hear.

I decided to do hypnosis, diving into that part of her that did not want to fully open up to David. When we are open and surrender to that higher part of ourselves, our minds have the intelligence to take us to the memory or experience that will shed light on what we are working on. I have seen this countless times with clients and with myself.

What emerged for Valerie was a history of disappointment and emotional abandonment, tracing back to her earliest experiences with her mother.

In hypnosis, Valerie stated, "Mom was supposed to come to the holiday sing-along at school. She never came."

"What did you come to believe when she didn't show up?" I asked.

"She's not interested in me. I don't matter," she said, lips quivering.

"Let's move forward a bit to the next time you felt you didn't matter," I said, guiding her forward.

"I came home from school crying because my friends left me out. They planned a sleepover without me," she sobbed.

"And what happened when you got home?" I asked.

"Mom brushed it off like it didn't matter! They were my friends, my only friends."

"Tell me what you came to believe."

"Mom doesn't care about me. My feelings don't matter. I don't matter." She slumped further into the couch and continued to sob.

Valerie's parents had a very volatile relationship while she was growing up, which can be unsettling to any child. One minute they would be affectionate with each other, and the next they would be having a shouting match.

"I never knew which version of Mom I would get. When things were good with her and Dad, she was actually nice. But when they weren't, watch out!" she said.

"Most of the time, I felt like an afterthought," she said, her lips turned downward. "My sister used to tell me what it was like when she was little. Mom would always show up for her school stuff, and when she got home from school, Mom would spend time with her and was interested in what she had to say," Valerie said, anger rising within her.

Tears streamed down her face. "I guess my sister was a better, more interesting person."

As a result of this dynamic, Valerie did not feel emotionally safe. She believed that life is scary and people can't be trusted. Due to her upbringing, Valerie also believed that she was alone and could only count on herself.

These beliefs stuck with her into adulthood and impacted her life, both positively and negatively. The positive thing was that, in believing that she was alone and could only count on herself, she made sure that she could support herself financially. She dedicated herself to her work, building a successful career. The negative was that she didn't let people in, and she didn't trust them. This left her feeling lonely, even when she was in a relationship.

When we have a belief, we subconsciously set out to prove it. Valerie proved the belief that she could not trust people by consistently choosing partners who let her down in one way or another. Upon further investigation, I found that her distrust of people spread into other relationships too. In particular, on the surface, she appeared to be very close to her cousin Nancy. They grew up together, and Valerie said she was like a sister to her. As she shared more about their relationship, it became clear that Nancy was not someone Valerie could count on for support.

When Valerie found out that David was still living with his wife, she turned to Nancy for support. Instead of offering a listening ear and support, Nancy chose to criticize Valerie. She brought up instances where Valerie had allowed others to take advantage of her and hurt her, spotlighting her past mistakes: the boyfriend who couldn't keep a steady job and the boyfriend who wouldn't commit. While Nancy's words contained some truth, in times of distress, dredging up past errors can cause emotional pain and promote a sense of shame.

While in a trance state, I guided Valerie to visualize the image of her younger self standing before her. She was able to feel her presence and energetically communicate with her. She spoke lovingly to her, saying, "I love you. You matter to me, and I am here for you. You are perfect exactly as you are."

Our continued work together focused on allowing Valerie's inner child to genuinely experience love, acknowledgment, care, and validation.

By creating an environment where her child self could feel seen, valued, and listened to, we were able to bridge the gap between intellectual understanding and heartfelt acceptance.

All of the memories, emotions, and thoughts of our past exist in the subconscious, and hypnosis provides access. We have the ability to rewire and shift our beliefs permanently. All that is required is a willingness and belief in the process. This is why people can quit smoking or change other behaviors through hypnosis.

It's essential to note that this process doesn't involve blaming Valerie's parents, as they genuinely loved her. However, due to her mother's preoccupation with the struggles in her marriage, she couldn't provide Valerie with the attention and time she needed as a six-year-old. Valerie's younger self interpreted this as a lack of love, importance, and worthiness, feeling that something was inherently wrong with her.

As an adult, Valerie could intellectually understand her mother's circumstances and empathize with her. Nevertheless, this understanding didn't necessarily shift the emotional perception of her child self. Our emotions, which operate subconsciously, hold a significant influence over our lives. In Valerie's case, although she recognized her mother's love and concern, her child self still held feelings of neglect.

As she connected with that part of herself, she heard, "Mom doesn't spend time with me. She would rather do other things, so there must be something wrong with me. I am not worth spending time with. I am not important. What I want doesn't matter."

I primarily use hypnosis to get to the false belief or story someone has accepted and then shift it. In Valerie's case, we uncovered the belief and its source, then shifted it by communicating with her child self. When she held her child self in her arms and asked her what she needed, the child said she wanted time and attention to feel loved.

Valerie's busy schedule currently didn't have much downtime, so the next step was to consciously build that time into her schedule.

I gave her the assignment to adjust her schedule and make time for herself. Valerie committed to taking a midday break rather than working through lunch every day. She actually found this helped her productivity.

She also planned at least one activity each week that was purely for pleasure; sometimes, it was as simple as spending an afternoon with a good book. The key to making the shift work is to do it consciously.

Valerie also shifted her self-talk; when she was doing something pleasurable or relaxing, she would say to herself, "This is for you, little one. I love you." This made her feel valued, and she continued to use this type of self-talk, especially when she was feeling insecure.

Valerie's other assignment was to meditate daily and have her child self sit with her in meditation. I recorded a guided meditation for her to assist her in this process. She decided to wake up 30 minutes earlier on workdays, allowing time for her to meditate and connect with her child self at the start of each day.

The shift that occurred in Valerie over the next couple of months was visible. She was more at peace with herself and calmer. Her facial muscles and posture became more relaxed. Her breathing pattern became slow and even. She had always been productive with her business, but now she was more relaxed and smiled more. Making time for herself was becoming more natural, and I could energetically sense the peace within her.

After several months, Valerie could sense that, despite his words and promises, David's actions showed he was not committed to their relationship. He was still living in the same house with his wife, with no progress toward getting his own place, and there was no movement toward his divorce. Even though she felt some sadness, she ended the relationship. She now knew that she deserved more from an intimate relationship.

Valerie went from accepting far less than 100% in her intimate relationships to deeply honoring herself and knowing her worth. She continues to connect with her child self in her daily meditation. She also prioritizes self-care and has shifted her schedule to reflect this prioritization. As she has come to know her worth, she feels confident that she will meet someone who shares her values and desire for a deep and meaningful relationship.

Journal prompt

- Have you ever settled for less than you desired in a relationship?
- If so, what did it look like in your experience?
- Imagine what might happen if you applied some of the techniques Valerie used to your life and write about it.

Chapter 12

Heart Shift Using Visualization, Affirmations, and Trust

Evan's Story

Evan walked into my office one day and complained of intense pain in his jaw. "The stress of this project is now causing me physical pain," he blurted as he threw his hands up in the air. Evan put his heart and soul into his work as a Risk Analyst for a risk management company. He was being pressured to submit a preliminary report about a hospital's ER department in an unrealistic time frame.

"The data is insufficient, and my manager is more concerned with getting it done than getting it right," he complained. Clearly, this went against everything Evan stood for. "I'm running myself ragged, working overtime, losing sleep, and I'm not even getting paid overtime for it. Why do I care so much?" he questioned.

After guiding him into a trance state, I said, "Place all your attention on your head, right where you're experiencing the pain. Energetically connect to that part of your body and imagine that you're sending beautiful, loving energy right there. Now, tune in and ask what this pain is trying to tell you."

"I see my wife," he immediately said. "She is so stressed, isn't sleeping well, and has these awful stomach aches. I can't seem to help her."

"Tell me more," I asked.

"I feel helpless. She knows I'm struggling right now, and I feel so guilty adding to her anxiety," he said, slumping down on the couch as he hunched his shoulders.

Our emotions are held in our bodies, and our bodies are always communicating with us. The question is: Are you listening? When a client comes to me with a physical symptom, I often use hypnosis to allow them to connect with and communicate with that part of the body.

In Evan's case, he realized that he was so focused on his wife's pain and the fact that he couldn't really help her that it was causing him physical pain. As he connected with his higher self, he sensed that visualizing her as empowered and engaging in the practices she uses to manage her anxiety would be helpful, so he did just that.

He began visualizing her doing her breathing exercises, yoga, and listening to music. As he did so, he began to relax, and the pain started to ease up.

"My worrying about her is actually causing her more stress," he said as he began to sit up a bit taller.

"What can you do to support her?" I asked.

"I can ask what she needs and remind her of the faith I have in her to get through this. In the past, I've taken on some of the things she normally does, and it's helped. I could do that without her having to ask," he said, sitting erect with his shoulders back.

By the time we finished the session, his pain was gone.

When he went home that evening, he suggested that they set aside the usual work tasks for the evening and spend 30 minutes going for a walk together. That one little tweak to the routine helped shift some energy. That evening, his wife was able to sleep peacefully through the night. It didn't change everything, but it was a start. Evan felt good about being part of the shift. More significantly, he knew that he couldn't "fix things" for her, and he knew he didn't have to be in pain as well. His role was to observe the situation and then ask her if she needed any support from him. After understanding her request, he would assess if he could fulfill it. If possible, he would then assist her to the best of his abilities. It was a matter of being supportive and loving, not taking responsibility for his wife's happiness. He understood that his dedication to being a compassionate partner did not mean he was responsible for her happiness, though he could support her in the process.

As Evan gained clarity around the physical pain and its connection to his wife, he was ready to dive back into the stress he was feeling at work. Not surprisingly, the two situations were related.

As we dove deeper into the situation, it was clear that Evan had a big story to share about the project.

"If I trust this incomplete data, I could make a mistake," Evan said, his voice angry and gruff.

"And then what happens?" I asked.

"I will be wrong."

"And if you're wrong?"

"They will think I am stupid," he said, dipping his head in shame.

"Who is 'they'?"

"My manager, the client, everyone!"

"Do you think you're stupid?"

Tears streamed down as he buried his face in his hands.

When the big emotion comes, the person has dropped from the conscious mind into the heart/gut and subconscious mind. I asked Evan to close his eyes and identify the emotion he was experiencing.

"I feel sad. And small," he said, tears still streaming down his face.

As I regressed him to the source of this sadness, the first time he had ever felt this way, he went back to an incident when he was in the first grade.

Evan was really excited about show and tell. He had his first Lego set, and he couldn't wait to show the class how he put it together. None of the other kids had anything like it. When he got up to show his Legos, the teacher stopped him.

"She told me the assignment was to find something in nature and talk about where I found it." He took a deep breath. "She told me I didn't listen to the instructions and made me sit down. I was so sad. I wanted to disappear."

Then he stated something that I instantly knew was the belief he took from this experience: "I was stupid for not following instructions."

As we explored this belief further, it became clear that this became a pattern in his life. Any time Evan made a mistake, even a small one, he felt stupid, and his internal dialogue reflected that feeling. In school, he put a lot of pressure on himself to excel. When he didn't get a perfect score, his focus was more on what he missed than what he got correct. This perfectionism led him to avoid trying some things due to the risk of failure.

For example, he loved math and wanted to be in the math club in junior high. He went back and forth, trying to decide if he should go for it. Ultimately, his fear of being stupid and the other kids knowing more than he did kept him from taking the leap.

He also came to realize that one of the reasons he felt so bad when he couldn't help his wife with her anxiety was because he felt stupid for not knowing what to do. Knowing his pattern of negative self-talk when he made a mistake helped him create a different story and begin his Heart Shift.

Since Evan had an analytical mind, I asked him to make a list of his accomplishments. His focus was so related to his mistakes that I wanted him to clearly see what his successes were. The challenge I gave him was to make a list of at least 100 things he had succeeded with. Once the list was made, he was to read it out loud twice a day.

A couple of weeks later, at our next session, he let me know that it was hard to get started with the list; however, once he got on a roll, he completed it quickly and read it out loud twice a day. Knowing Evan's desire to do things right, I was not surprised he completed the task assigned. Evan was pleased with the shift he began to feel.

"After several days, I noticed that I started feeling different, more positive," he said.

"How so?" I asked.

"I was really busy at work and missed a couple of days working out.

Normally, I get down on myself when I let that go because it is really matters to me. This time, I was so much more accepting and kinder to myself in my head," he said. "I knew I would start right back."

Our next step was to take things deeper into the subconscious, where permanent change happens.

In hypnosis, I read part of the list of successes to him. His brow and facial muscles softened as a gentle smile formed. After reading the list, I asked him what he knew to be true about himself, and he stated the following:

"I am smart."

"I am compassionate."

"I try my best in all I do."

"I am a good person."

I wrote down his exact words and instructed him to repeat these affirmations to himself daily until our next session. This was when his self-talk started to shift. He felt optimistic about the future, and when something didn't go as planned, he found it easier to let go.

When Evan arrived for his next session, he looked more relaxed and at peace than I had ever seen him. He was smiling, his head was held high, and he was not fidgeting as he typically did. As expected, he completed the assignment I gave him. He also shared with me that he had finished the preliminary report at work. Although he wasn't totally confident it was all correct, he felt okay with it.

"It was like a lightbulb went off in my head," he said. "It was preliminary, and there would not necessarily be immediate actions taken on the report. I found myself saying things in my head like, *It's okay, you're doing your best. It doesn't have to be perfect. You're smart.*"

He felt a renewed sense of trust, accepting that not everything had to be perfect. He also stated that he felt almost silly when he thought about how worked up he would get.

Evan was determined to continue his progress and release the burden of trying to be perfect. With this new outlook, he was beginning to embrace the challenge of trying new things. He started experimenting with cooking, searching for recipes, and trying different cuisines. Not all the dishes were a success. The first time he tried making pizza, the crust burnt. The second time, the crust was soggy. The third time, it was a success—crispy and delicious.

The biggest success of all was that he didn't get down on himself for his mistakes. He was able to laugh it off and try again. He came to love cooking and modifying recipes to make them his own.

His passion for cooking brought an unexpected benefit. His wife was generally the one who cooked. When he took on the responsibility for cooking most nights, she was able to have a break for herself after work, which was a great reliever for her stress.

Once Evan eased up on himself, things seemed to get easier at work, too. Our thoughts and feelings can have a direct influence on our reality. He had made an energetic shift, and when we do this, things around us tend to change, too. This is a prime example of a Heart Shift.

Evan went from perfectionism and believing he was stupid to feeling empowered and relaxed. The use of affirmations and visualization enabled him to trust himself more fully, embrace his strengths, and let go of taking on too much responsibility, creating his Heart Shift.

Journal prompt

- Do you have physical pain or discomfort? Breathe into the discomfort and sense what your body is trying to tell you.

You'll find the "Listen to Your Body" hypnosis in the book portal to support your inquiry.

Chapter 13

Heart Shift Using Forgiveness and Self-love

Maggie's Story

WHEN MAGGIE WALKED into my office for the first time, the atmosphere seemed to subtly shift, as if the room itself could sense the heaviness she carried. Each step she took seemed to require a great deal of effort, as if she were wading through a swamp of her own despair.

Maggie sat down and took a deep breath. "My boyfriend cheated on me with my best friend," she blurted, immediately breaking into sobs. It was clear this was the culmination of many years of betrayal—the last straw that finally led her to seek help.

She stated that it was her third significant relationship that had ended in shambles. She felt completely dejected and hopeless, fearing she would never find the love and connection she desperately desired. Although each relationship was slightly different, they all ended with her finding out her partner had deceived her in some way. Maggie could not understand why this kept happening. She was always honest and forthright with her partners, which was rarely reciprocated.

"Tell me what life was like for you growing up," I prompted.

As Maggie shared her story with me and spoke about her family dynamics growing up, it was evident that her family did not model the kind of relationship she desired. Her parents split up when she was young, and their relationship while together was very tumultuous.

"My mom cheated on Dad, and they had terrible fights about it. I would wake up in the middle of the night to their fighting, and I couldn't escape. I remember getting under the covers and wrapping my pillow around my head, trying to silence the yelling. There was no escaping it."

As Maggie shared her experience, tears began rolling down her cheeks, and her voice trembled.

In exploring Maggie's emotions around her most recent failed relationship, a lot of self-blame and shame came up.

"I never should have trusted either one of them!" she exclaimed. "I've never been able to keep a man and never will." She covered her face and sobbed.

I suspected there was more going on than simply repeating patterns she had experienced and witnessed growing up. While there was no tangible evidence to support the suspicion, I intuitively felt it. It was a calm certainty that washed over me and told me there was more.

While in hypnosis, Maggie recalled the experience of being sexually molested by her older cousin when she was five years old. Afterward, she immediately told her mother, who didn't believe her and brushed it off as a figment of her imagination.

When trauma is experienced and someone recalls it in hypnosis, it's paramount not to retraumatize the person by having them relive the specifics. What is necessary to uncover is what happens after the trauma—what one comes to believe about themselves, about the situation, and about life.

Often, in the case of sexual abuse in particular, one can in some way blame themselves or think they did something wrong. Self-blame can then exacerbate the emotional pain and contribute to feelings of shame, guilt, and PTSD. Children who experience sexual abuse can be especially prone to self-blame due to their limited understanding of power dynamics. The fact that Maggie's mother did not believe her magnified these emotions.

As we proceeded with the hypnosis, it was clear that Maggie not only blamed herself but believed that she was making "a big deal out of nothing."

As she spoke of the abuse, she stated, "I should have pushed him away or screamed," and "It only happened once." Because of her mother's reaction, she diminished the impact it had on her. It was almost like Maggie took her mother's side as opposed to taking a stand for her younger self.

During the hypnosis, I supported her in sending loving energy and compassion to her child self. Once she came out of hypnosis, we had a conversation about the abuse.

"I get that I couldn't stop him. He was bigger and stronger," she said.

At that point, Maggie could logically and intellectually see that what happened was wrong and not her fault. The driving issue is always the subconscious belief, and her child self still held the belief that she did something wrong. Our work was to shift the subconscious to match the intellectual belief.

For the next several sessions, I gently guided Maggie, while in trance, to form a deep bond with her five-year-old self. Her child self needed to be heard. This part of herself believed: "No one believes me. What I say doesn't matter. I am not loved. I am not good enough."

I encouraged Maggie to energetically ask her child self what she needed to feel safe, cared for, and heard. She sensed that the busyness of her schedule left little time for the relaxation and creativity that the child needed. As Maggie practiced tuning in to her intuition through daily meditation, she gained the strength to say "no" more often and prioritize her well-being. At the time, Maggie was pretty much a workaholic, which left little time for self-care.

When you don't feel you are enough and are not loved, you tend to overcompensate by overworking. This is exactly what Maggie had done. She excessively over-gave her time at work to feel valued and useful. Realizing this, one of the decisions she made was to leave work on time most nights and have a date night with herself once a week. On these date nights, she did things purely for the joy of it. Some of the activities included watching funny movies, drawing, and journaling. She enjoyed drawing so much that she decided to take an art class.

Maggie also prioritized self-care and love by ensuring she got enough sleep, encouraged physical activity, and maintained healthy eating habits. She noticed her energy increase as she adopted these new habits.

Over the course of a few months, her life began to shift. One aspect that surprised her was that her work did not suffer despite spending less time on it. Since she was rested and happier, she was able to work more efficiently and get more done in less time. She also noticed that she felt much more positive about her future.

"I actually see myself in a loving relationship," she said. "I'm starting to feel exhilarated about building a life that has me excited to get out of bed in the morning!"

It may seem simple, but it was crucial for Maggie to get comfortable practicing loving acts of self-care to begin shifting the false belief around her worth and value as a human being. When we take care of ourselves, we're sending a message that we matter. The effects of this are boundless.

Entering a relationship when you fully know your worth empowers you to make good choices for yourself and attract a partner who values you. Maggie wanted to be in a relationship and have children. Although she was feeling better about herself, she was anxious about dating due to her previous relationships. Our next step was to examine those previous relationships and look for any clues she may have overlooked early on, which could have warned her of what was to come.

People show their true selves to us—sometimes overtly and other times subtly. It's not uncommon to overlook the negatives until they escalate, such as discovering a partner's infidelity. Reflecting on the past is a way to identify these signs. This isn't about self-blame; instead, it's about harvesting the wisdom for future benefit. Examining past experiences in this way empowers us to know for certain what warrants our attention. In doing so, Maggie would gain confidence moving forward into her next relationship.

Maggie's most recent relationship was with Paul. He was charming and charismatic and captured Maggie's heart quickly. Using hypnotherapy, we explored the early times of their relationship, looking for clues to the eventual cheating.

Maggie remembered being struck by his need for constant validation and attention from others. He consistently sought external approval. When they were out, he would often speak loudly to draw attention to himself or strike up conversations with strangers at a bar and buy them drinks to appear generous. It was a potential red flag, which at the time she saw as an expression of his outgoing personality.

Another sign she pushed down was his tendency to keep certain aspects of his life private, even though they had become remarkably close and spoke often of their future together. While he appeared open and transparent about his family, he rarely shared anything about his work or colleagues. He always kept his phone under wraps, never letting it out of his sight. He even brought it into the bathroom with him. Maggie interpreted this as his commitment to being available for clients and staying on top of things with his business.

As time went on, Maggie noticed lapses in communication and unexplained absences. She believed his excuses about late work meetings and last-minute deadlines because, for the most part, she trusted him. As she described this to me, she remembered it was around this time she started experiencing headaches.

As I previously shared, our bodies are always speaking to us. I knew Maggie's headaches were telling her something was wrong. Somewhere, there was a disconnect between what was actually happening and what she wanted to see and believe.

In hypnosis, I guided her to energetically connect with her head. "Imagine each breath you're taking is flowing into your head," I said. "And imagine that your heart is flowering open and all the loving energy that exists in your heart is now flowing into your head. Feel the warmth and comfort of it."

As Maggie relaxed and felt the peace of that loving energy enfolding and surrounding her head, I instructed her to go back to a time when

Paul was absent or uncommunicative. As she did so, she began to have a headache. It was clear that the discrepancy between what she was witnessing and what she wanted to believe was literally giving her headaches.

At this point, it was imperative for her to understand why she had not confronted Paul or taken a stand for herself. She knows now that he was having an affair, and there is no need for self-blame regarding how long she stayed with him. The goal is to harvest the learning so the pain is not repeated.

Maggie realized that her beliefs ("No one believes me. What I say doesn't matter. I am not loved. I am not good enough.") were what held her back from confronting Paul. She didn't want her fears to be true. If he was cheating, it reconfirmed that she wasn't good enough. ("What if I was wrong? What if my accusation pushes him away? What if I never find the relationship I so desperately desire?") It's no wonder the inner conflict and turmoil caused headaches!

While in hypnosis, I asked, "Knowing what you know now, what do you believe about yourself? What do you believe about life?"

She was very clear that there was absolutely no blame that should be placed on her due to the abuse and the fact that her mother did not believe her. She knew she was a good person who deserved to be treated well.

"I was an innocent child," she said. "The person who was supposed to protect me didn't. There was nothing more I could have done."

Up to this point, Maggie had been reluctant to speak about the fact that there was another betrayal. This was the betrayal of her friend Lindsay, who had the affair with Paul. They hadn't spoken since Maggie found out, although Lindsay reached out on multiple occasions, begging for forgiveness.

"I will never forgive her. What she did was unforgivable," Maggie told me through tears.

Maggie had recurring nightmares about Paul and Lindsay laughing at her. Thoughts of what they had done tormented her on a regular basis. Maggie had come so far, and yet this felt like too much.

As I shared in my chapter on forgiveness, true forgiveness has nothing to do with the person or thing you are forgiving. It is about releasing your emotional connection to them.

I let Maggie know, "It is all about you and freeing yourself from the toxic energy of the situation. Holding on to anger and hate will keep you emotionally connected to Lindsay."

"Well, I certainly don't want to be connected to her," she responded.

I further explained, "Forgiveness doesn't mean what she did was okay or that you have to be friends with her. What it does mean is that you let go of the pain and free yourself to live and move forward."

Maggie was initially skeptical when I explained this to her; however, we had built a good rapport over the time we worked together, and she was willing to explore what forgiveness might feel like. Fortunately, all it takes is a willingness to get started.

Over the course of several sessions, I worked with Maggie, guiding her through my four-step process of forgiveness.

Step One: Feel and express all your feelings.

When we bottle up our emotions, they often spill out in the wrong moments and toward the wrong people.

For example, due to the hurt over Lindsay's betrayal, Maggie was mistrustful of the other people in her life. At one point, she overheard a conversation between coworkers and was convinced they were talking about her. She became noticeably quiet and withdrawn. When a coworker asked what was wrong, she tearfully stated that she had heard their conversation and knew that they thought she was not very good in her role as assistant manager. As it turned out, the coworkers were talking about a reality TV show.

For step one of forgiveness, Maggie was hesitant to express anger. As a child, the fighting between her parents was very frightening. Because of this, she avoided confrontation and resisted anger at all costs.

We discussed healthy ways for Maggie to express her anger, and she began expressing her feelings by writing, which felt the most comfortable and unthreatening to her. Her homework assignment was to write about the hurt and betrayal that she felt, specifically regarding her friend.

"Lindsay broke the girl code. You don't mess around with your friend's boyfriend," she wrote. "If I can't trust my girlfriends, who can I trust?"

Maggie discovered that by writing her feelings out and releasing them on paper, she was able to get some relief. The anger would build up, she would cry, and then it would settle down.

Oftentimes, physical movement can also be an effective way to release the energy of that anger. So, in addition to writing and allowing the tears to flow, I encouraged her to do some cardio exercises or try hitting a pillow with a tennis racket or screaming into a pillow when she was angry. All of these activities can help us channel our anger and tap into the deeper emotions beneath it, which, in this case, were feelings of sadness and disappointment.

Anger is often a surface reaction, a kind of emotional shield that protects us from facing our more vulnerable feelings. It can feel easier and safer to express anger than to admit to ourselves or others that we are deeply hurt or afraid.

Maggie found it particularly satisfying to yell into a pillow, as she had not really used her voice to speak up for herself in the past. As time went on, the writing shifted from accusations about Lindsay to Maggie's feelings about herself and the pain of the betrayal. Ultimately, she wrote, "Nobody really cares about me. I simply don't matter."

Her friend's betrayal hit a nerve, reactivating the pain of her mother not believing her about the abuse. Realizing this connection, the intensity of the anger toward Lindsay began to diminish.

A wise teacher once told me that when we journal, the key is to hold on to the insights, a-ha moments, goals, dreams, and all of the good that has happened—and release the pain, trauma, and negative emotions.

To hold onto the good, Maggie's next assignment was to go over what she had written, harvest the learning from it, and write that in her journal.

She wrote, "The betrayal of my friend triggered the hurt of my mom not believing me about the abuse. This caused a spiral of intense pain. My friend betrayed me, and I am okay. I have the ability to move through this. I am not a child who doesn't know where to turn. I have resources."

Maggie's self-confidence was already beginning to resurface.

To release the bad, Maggie's next assignment was to take the writings about the pain and, in the way of her choosing, destroy them, signifying the release of the anger. There is something powerful about ritual, as it impresses the subconscious.

For instance, when my first marriage ended, I saw my move into an apartment by myself as a fresh beginning. I was determined not to carry the emotional baggage from my past relationship into this new space. The timing felt perfect; it was New Year's Eve, a moment that naturally invites transformation. I decided to perform a ritual. In the glow of candlelight, tears streaming down my face, I wrote down everything I wanted to release—the memories, the emotional strain, and the residual pain I was holding on to.

As I read through what I had written, I was highly aware of the energy of all the burdens I had been carrying. I lit the paper on fire and watched it burn down to ashes. As the paper turned to smoke, I felt as if all my pain was dissolving with it.

While this act was symbolic, it was not the only thing I did to heal. I had already done considerable work to process the anger, hurt, and disappointment that I felt throughout the ending of my marriage. Even so, this ritual served as a significant culminating step in my journey of letting go and was a deeply powerful moment for me.

Together, Maggie and I devised a plan for her release. She was going to release on the full moon, which was a week away. It is said that the full moon's energy is one of completion and transformation, which makes it a great time to release that which is no longer serving you.

Maggie waited until dark, lit some candles out on her patio, and spoke an intention about releasing the past and moving forward. She then, page by page, burned her writings about the anger. As each sheet caught fire, the flames consumed the words, turning them into a display of orange and red sparks. With each page she burned, she envisioned the anger leaving her body, its smoky remnants rising and dissipating into the air. Although there was more forgiveness work to do, Maggie was already feeling a little lighter.

Then, we moved on to step two.

Step Two: Break it down to only the facts

There are facts, and there are the stories we tell ourselves. Speaking only facts without inserting any judgments or emotions can be a challenge. Think of it this way: if someone were observing the interaction or circumstance from the outside, what would they see and hear?

When Maggie first told me the story of what happened between Paul and Lindsay, it went something like this: "He had the nerve to lie and deceive me, breaking my heart while messing around with my friend. She betrayed our friendship. She's a cheat and a liar. She doesn't care about me, and she never cared about our friendship. She is selfish."

Although it felt emotionally true, most of these statements are assumptions. Maggie has no way of knowing whether Lindsay doesn't care about their friendship or doesn't respect her or care about her feelings. Those statements may or may not be true.

As Maggie broke it down to just the facts, she stated, "Lindsay and Paul had an intimate relationship while I was in what I thought was a committed relationship with Paul."

This is not to say that what Lindsay and Paul did together had not impacted Maggie—of course, it did. She was devastated. It is simply to state the fact that they did what they did, and only Lindsay and Paul know their true motivations and intentions.

This step continues to release emotion around the person or circumstance by turning the focus from story to facts. It further serves as a reminder if Maggie begins to get into the victim story again. She can remind herself of the facts and halt the telling of the story. While there is certainly emotion in the facts, the stories we make up around those facts carry the bigger emotions, and that's what we're trying to release in this step.

Step Three: Flip it. What if the opposite were true?

In Maggie's case, she was devastated by her friend's betrayal. But what if there is something that Maggie can find within the situation that could benefit her?

We did hypnosis around this possibility to tap into Maggie's higher self. She came to realize several useful things: if not with her friend, Paul might have cheated on her with someone else. Maggie also learned that Lindsay wasn't someone she could trust. In hindsight, she recalled the ways Lindsay had not been completely truthful, like gossiping behind people's backs and making up lies to avoid doing something. She also recognized that the devastation she felt due to the betrayal caused her to seek help and get to the root of some long-standing issues.

Was Maggie happy about the suffering? No, of course not. What she was happy about was digging in and harvesting the learning from it. She is stronger and wiser because of what she has gone through.

This step provides perspective. When we own our part and examine how the situation may have benefited us, we shift from being a victim to being empowered. We also know what to pay attention to in the future to protect ourselves. We don't have to put up walls; we can simply filter out what does not serve us.

Step Four: Own It

This one can be a bit tricky, especially for someone like Maggie, who had a long-standing relationship with self-blame due to her childhood trauma. But blaming is different from taking responsibility.

Self-blame is a critical and negative evaluation of oneself that can result in feelings of guilt, shame, low self-esteem, anxiety, and depression. It focuses on the past, fixating on faults or mistakes, and is generally unproductive and harmful.

Taking responsibility for oneself, on the other hand, involves acknowledging one's actions, recognizing their consequences, and then focusing on learning, growth, and making amends where necessary.

In Maggie's case, it was her beliefs ("No one believes me. What I say doesn't matter. I am not loved. I am not good enough.") that attracted a friend who would betray her and a partner who would cheat on her. Subconsciously, we set out to prove our beliefs, even the false ones.

When someone takes responsibility, they are owning their part in a situation with the understanding that they can choose different actions in the future. This fosters personal growth, self-improvement, and resilience. Taking responsibility is future-focused, as it involves formulating a plan to avoid repeating past mistakes and to act differently moving forward.

Maggie continued to reflect on her friendship with Lindsay and the pattern of small deceptions. Several times during their friendship, Lindsay canceled plans with an excuse that Maggie later found out was not true. She also often told Maggie confidential information about mutual friends. She realized that these, and a few other things, were all indicators that Lindsay was not someone she could trust.

By identifying these patterns, Maggie is now empowered to be more observant in future relationships and make choices about whom to trust from a place of confidence and trust in herself.

In the past, Maggie subconsciously did not feel good enough or lovable enough to have a loyal, honest friend. It was not her fault—it was her conditioning and belief system. Fortunately, through dedication and commitment, as well as through self-love and forgiveness, Maggie is now clear that she deserves love, honesty, and people in her life who respect her.

I am happy to say that although Maggie's friendship with Lindsay is over, she has forgiven her. By working through the steps, she was able to gain a new perspective on the relationship. She took ownership of her part (ignoring warning signs) and came to understand that holding onto the anger only served to keep her connected to Lindsay.

Maggie also worked through the steps and forgave Paul. Although their relationship ended when she uncovered the infidelity, it was finally through forgiveness that she was able to move on and focus on what she desired: a loving, committed relationship.

Maggie went from anger, self-blame, and mistrust to confidently stepping into her power. She feels confident that the relationship she desires, including having children, is not only possible but probable. In learning to love and care for herself and forgive those who have harmed her, she has experienced a Heart Shift and is joyously moving forward.

Journal prompt

- What patterns do you notice in your personal relationships and/or employment?
- As you reflect on these patterns, make note of any warning signs you may have previously ignored.

Chapter 14

Heart Shift Using Visioning, Visualization, and Meditation

Wendy's Story

WENDY STOOD AT the precipice of a major life decision, ready to leave her uninspiring job at a nonprofit and embark on a career using her creativity as a children's book author and illustrator. Just as the decisive moment approached and she was about to give notice to her employer, she became paralyzed by fear. This was when she reached for an emergency session to uncover what brought her to this place of intense fear.

When she walked into my office that day, her face was filled with tension, and she nervously clutched her purse. She spoke rapidly about the fear that had gripped her.

"I don't think I can do this. What if I fail? What if I can't pay my bills and lose my home?" Wendy fired off in rapid succession, tears welling up in her eyes.

This was not the Wendy who walked out of my office a few weeks earlier. That Wendy was confident, ready to take the next step and live her dream.

Wendy had initially come to see me to work on her general dissatisfaction with her job. She held a leadership position in a nonprofit. Although she felt connected to the mission, she did not feel a strong connection to the work she was doing. She had always been creative, enjoying the process of writing stories and illustrating them. In our work together, we realized that although she loved creativity, she had a belief in the starving artist's story.

You know the one—you could be creative, or you could be successful. You can have money or do work you love. That type of thing. She did not believe that she could earn a living and support herself doing work that she loved.

Through hypnotherapy, we were previously able to uncover this belief and see that it came from her family of origin. Her family believed that once you get a job, you stick with working for a good, solid company, and you stay in that job until the day you retire. Her family had all taken that path and it hadn't led to much joy for any of them. Wendy wanted something different, but she didn't know how to achieve it.

We began doing visioning and getting an idea of the essence and feel of what she wanted to create. The more we visioned and she allowed her soul to speak to her, the more clarity she received around what she really wanted to do—write and illustrate children's stories.

As I described in the chapter on visioning, it involves asking a series of questions in a meditative state and listening to the higher wisdom that comes through. During the process, I asked Wendy what the highest vision for the work she was here to do was; she had vivid, colorful images.

"I see rainbows, flowers, fairies, and unicorns. There's so much joy and brightness in these images. I feel a sense of freedom and excitement," she declared with a huge smile on her face.

"And what do you need to empower this cheerful vision?" I asked.

"I hear the words freedom and flexibility."

"What needs to be released to manifest the vision?"

"I see my dad coming home from work tired and complaining about how much he hates his job. Mom was no happier with hers. They never did anything to try and change it. I cannot—no, I will not—allow myself to be like that," she emphatically stated.

Wendy was abundantly clear that she wanted to do work that brought her joy, was a positive contribution to the world, and allowed time for solitude and for her loved ones. She always treasured her time alone as it recharged her. When her schedule was full and she did not have time with herself to get reenergized, she found that she was less productive and more irritable.

The pandemic had an impact on her that she didn't fully realize until we started exploring that balance between alone time and being out in the world. She had always been somewhat of a loner, and during the pandemic, she was very isolated since she lived alone and worked from home. She fell into a very comfortable rhythm of being only with herself for days on end.

While it may have been necessary for a while, the truth was that she missed being with people, and she found it difficult to jump back in. During her time in isolation, her creativity was heightened. Ideas for stories and the images that went with them flowed freely. Wendy shared one of her stories with her parents.

Her dad said, "Why are you wasting time with that? There's no money in it. Focus on your job."

Her mom had a similar reaction. "What's the point, Wendy? It may be a fun little hobby, but if you work a little harder at your job, maybe you'll get a promotion."

Those reactions, coupled with her own insecurities, led Wendy to keep her writing to herself, although she secretly hoped it could be a new career.

The visioning we did gave Wendy inspiration to start exploring the opportunity to do something she felt passionate about. She had always thought that writing and illustrating children's stories on an online platform would be a terrific way to reach children by sending a positive message, and that was exactly what she did.

Wendy started a YouTube channel to share her stories, and within a few months, she had a strong online presence and many followers. She even had a couple of advertisers supplement the subscription fee that people paid. Wendy quickly reached a point where, in order to continue to grow and expand her business, she needed more time, which meant her day job had to go. She was all set to give notice to her employer. It was all so clear, and yet she was paralyzed by her fear.

When she arrived for the emergency session, I could feel the pain and tension in her energy. The tears flowed almost immediately.

Through her sobs, she cried out, "What am I doing? I can't do this! I must be crazy thinking I could go through with this."

That's when the "what ifs" started.

"What if I can't pay my mortgage or health insurance? What if the sponsors back out? What if I choke and can't write?"

"What if you are a huge success?" I countered. "What if even more sponsors want to support what you are doing?"

As she began to take some of my "what ifs" into consideration, her breathing became less shallow, and her gripped fists loosened.

I explained the concept called "second crop" that I learned in my Spiritual Practitioner training. Second crop is something that can come up after you shift a false or limiting belief and things in your life start to change. You are moving forward, happier, and more of your true self. Then something happens—maybe you start a new relationship or job, whatever it may be—and the false or limiting belief you moved past rears its ugly head once again.

This was what was happening to Wendy. She had worked toward this goal, felt ready, and planned for it, and then the fear took over.

While this can temporarily stop or halt progress, it is merely a bump in the road, not a boulder or some insurmountable obstacle. It is central to remember that the truths we embrace as we release false and limiting beliefs require ongoing attention, much like a blossoming garden. This is why spiritual practices such as meditation, visioning, and affirmations are so vital.

If you're a tennis player, you practice your serve. You volley back and forth and engage in running or strength training. If you stopped practicing and exercising, your game would suffer.

Shifting our beliefs from those we adopted at an early age and have lived with for some time is not necessarily a one-and-done process. Once you expand the mind, it never goes back to what it was. However, to really strengthen it and not waver, it is crucial to continue the practice.

Whether the practice is reading inspiring books, listening to podcasts, or having deep conversations with people, all of these things support us in staying focused on what we're creating in our lives and how we desire to continue to live.

"Tell me about what you have been doing to prepare for leaving your job," I questioned.

"I practiced what I'm going to say to my boss. I've been setting aside a little extra money from every paycheck and researching additional potential sponsors," she said without emotion.

"What about your meditation practice, journaling, and listening to inspirational podcasts?" I asked.

"Well," she paused, head hanging down a little, "I've been kind of busy for all that stuff, so I haven't been doing it every day."

In our previous work together, meditation and journaling had been integral parts of her journey. She had developed a morning practice of listening to something inspirational as she got ready for the day, sitting down and journaling about what was coming up for her, then meditating for 20 minutes.

For months, she did this every day, and it helped her stay connected to her vision and what was possible. Wendy shared that, in preparation for leaving her job, she had been too busy to meditate, and journaling had become only an occasional thing.

I felt that Wendy had lost some of the passion for what she was doing, and as her focus wavered, the fear and "what ifs" began to creep in. I knew it was vital for her to get back in touch with her higher why for what she was doing; she wanted to do work that brought her joy and made a difference in people's lives. I guided her through a visualization of what she was building for her life and her work.

After taking a few conscious breaths and allowing herself to become grounded, I asked Wendy to imagine that she had left her job and was writing and illustrating stories full-time. I asked her to use all of her senses to imagine it.

"I feel a tingling sensation all over," Wendy said. "The excitement is palpable. I'm seeing more sponsors reaching out. I'm picturing the faces of the children as they read the stories and look at the drawings. They're getting the messages that I'm bringing to them through my stories. My stories matter; they make a difference. They bring not only joy, but they carry deeper messages about friendship, sharing, and being kind."

As she spoke, her energy had completely shifted. I could see the excitement rising within her. She was sitting a little taller, had become more animated, and had a big smile on her face. By the time we completed the visualization, Wendy felt like a weight had been lifted.

Wendy's assignment was to allow herself to visualize what she was creating on a daily basis. Even five minutes a day would be enough to keep that vision alive and pull her forward. I made a recording for her to listen to that would support the visualization.

Although she had approached the day she planned to give notice to her employer, she decided to hold off for a few more weeks to bolster the confidence and strength she felt at that moment.

Wendy recommitted to the practices that had gotten her to the point of being ready to step into her new career. She scheduled her daily meditation, journaling, and visualization practice. To hold herself accountable, she reached out to a close friend and asked her to be an accountability buddy. Overall, Wendy had a great plan to move forward.

When Wendy came to my office a couple of weeks later, she was back to her confident self. She had quickly bounced back to where she had been a couple of months prior. I could see it in the way she walked into my office, the smile on her face, and her erect posture. It was a great reminder to her of why she had chosen to do the practices and had made the commitments she had to herself.

Often, when we embrace new habits, things start to fall into place. We may find ourselves enjoying more satisfaction from our careers or relationships. However, we sometimes relax and let go of these new practices, forgetting their integral role in our improved situation. When this happens, we can experience a second crop. It is something that happens to many of us, myself included. The key thing is that we notice it and take action to shift it.

I tell my clients, "When you realize you've fallen back into an old pattern or way of thinking, it's actually a good thing. We cannot change what we don't recognize, so be happy you recognized it and know the steps you need to take to get back on track."

Wendy felt ready to step forward and give her two-week notice to her employer. The slight setback and delay had actually made her stronger. The fear she experienced reminded her of how she had previously felt when she didn't have hope, a plan, or a dream for what she wanted to create in her life. She had more determination than ever to move forward with her plan and build her new career, and that is exactly what she did.

As I write this, Wendy is a couple of months into writing and illustrating children's books full-time and is loving it. She feels a tremendous sense of satisfaction in putting something out into the world that can benefit people. Also, she is overjoyed at the fact that she gets to do something she loves!

It doesn't mean it's always easy or that she's not working hard. It means she's doing something that matters, and she's loving it. She continues to prioritize her meditation and journaling practice. Wendy's Heart Shift has her well on her way to fulfilling her desire to be of service to others while living a joyous and abundant life for herself.

Journal prompt

Reflect on a time when you were making strides toward a personal goal or intention and then experienced a setback.

- What steps can you take to rekindle your passion and regain the momentum that fueled your initial progress?

Chapter 15

Heart Shift Using
Self- Love and Affirmations

Gary's Story

WHEN GARY WALKED into my office for the first time, he sat down—shoulders slumped, head hanging down, and arms crossed. According to him, he was a victim of circumstances. Technology never worked for him; he was always having trouble with his computer. Whether it was getting online to pay bills or whatever else he needed to do, there was always some problem. At work, everyone else could easily navigate various programs, but when he tried, there was always an issue. Gary was in a very strong victim story.

I asked him to share a little bit about what life was like growing up. He lived in a two-parent household with three older brothers.

"Mom was the boss. If she was upset or demanding something, everyone jumped! We would do anything to keep the peace, and it wasn't easy," he said.

"Tell me more," I instructed.

"I never really felt like I belonged—I'm different than my brothers and my parents," he said, head down.

Gary shared that he loved art and creative pursuits, whereas his brothers excelled in academics and were far more analytical, like his parents. Academically, Gary struggled. He worked very hard to earn good grades, and although his grades were perfectly acceptable, they were not the A+'s his brothers got.

Gary's mother compared him to his brothers, saying, "Why can't you be more like Steve? He got an A on his chemistry test." And "Ben always gets his work done on time and never seems to struggle. Why do you always mess up on the computer?"

As soon as Gary graduated from high school, he packed up and moved across the country to get as far away as he could from his family. Unlike his brothers, he did not seek higher education in the traditional form. Gary became a yoga instructor, and while he enjoyed the work, he longed for more. He had a dream of opening his own studio. But every time he thought about doing it, his self-doubt and victimhood came crashing down.

He threw his hands in the air and told me, "How can I even think about opening my own studio when I can't even manage the scheduling system at the studio where I work now?"

We began our work together with a simple and gentle process to connect him with his higher self. It was clear that Gary had built up a wall of protection around himself. When he spoke of his childhood and the way his mother spoke to him, there was no emotion. His face was blank, as if he were numb.

When we build walls, we not only block what we are trying to protect ourselves from, but we also block the good. When one has been hurt, especially by their primary caretaker, the beliefs that are adopted as a result are commonly those of worthlessness, self-loathing, shame, and a general lack of self-love. Gary believed: "I can't do computer stuff because I'm not smart enough. I'll never be as successful as my brothers. I'm a disappointment and embarrassment to my family."

Even today, Gary's mother consistently compares him to his older brothers. While they were each unique in their own way, they all did well academically and went on to higher education. They also had careers that Gary's mother felt were more suitable than being a yoga instructor. Gary's accomplishments were never valued or celebrated—and he did have accomplishments!

He was one of his area's most loved yoga instructors. His classes were always full. The studio owner held him in high regard, and his salary exceeded that of the other instructors. Unfortunately for Gary, none of this impressed his family, especially his mother.

We had to move slowly for Gary to become more open and let that wall down a bit so we could see what was going on. In early sessions, we practiced putting up a filter of protection. A filter allows the good in but filters out the hurtful energy. Practicing thinking of his protection as a filter rather than a wall helped Gary see that there were people around him who were there to support him and love him. The wall he had put up was impacting not only intimate relationships but friendships.

While he was in a trance, I guided Gary to connect with his heart and the loving energy within.

"Now imagine this beautiful, loving energy pouring out of your heart and filling your entire body. Feel the warmth and comfort of it as it fills you completely," I said. "Imagine that loving energy extending out beyond your body as if you are in a bubble of love."

I could see Gary's shoulders drop and his facial muscles relax as he leaned back and breathed deeply. He felt the safety and comfort of that loving energy, and I let him know that the energy bubble was a filter allowing only loving energy in. I recorded this process for him so that he could listen to it regularly and become more comfortable letting the wall down and trusting the filter.

As Gary became more comfortable, I regressed him to childhood, where he had several memories, as young as three years old, of his mother saying things like:

- "You are stupid."
- "You can't get anything right."
- "Why can't you be like your brothers?"

While in the trance, Gary was right there emotionally, experiencing the pain of those words. Tears rolled down his cheeks, his body curled forward, shrinking into the couch as if he were being swallowed up in pain. He came to understand that this was when he first believed that he couldn't do anything right and that there was something wrong with him.

When someone is experiencing a significant amount of emotional pain, I always check in and give them the option to pull out of the pain and become an observer of the situation.

"I'm okay," Gary assured me.

Experiencing it helped him to identify and become very clear about the beliefs he adopted because of his mother's words.

As I have said before, when we have false beliefs, we subconsciously set out to prove them. We can intellectually be aware that we are not worthless, that we are, in fact, valuable, and that we do, in fact, have skills and many wonderful qualities. However, if the underlying subconscious belief is "I am not good enough," then that is what's really running the show.

This is why hypnosis is so powerful. We can access the subconscious mind and change the belief at the source. This is exactly what my work with Gary focused on.

As Gary heard those words from his mother and experienced the sadness and shame he felt as a young boy, he again felt the pain and identified what he came to believe:

- "I am stupid."
- "I can't do anything right."
- "I'll never be as smart or successful as my brothers."

I then inquired what behaviors Gary had adopted in his life because of believing he was stupid, couldn't do anything right, and would never be as smart and successful as his brothers.

"I spent little time playing with friends and didn't have many connections with other children. I was a loner," he said. "I stay in the background and am a follower rather than a leader, even when I have good ideas."

Even now, at the yoga studio, he could see how, although he had a great deal of expertise, he would never speak up at staff meetings, even when he had ideas. He never considered higher education because he believed he would fail. The belief that he was stupid also kept him from opening his own yoga studio.

At this point in the process, the pain Gary was feeling was intense. His voice was quivering, his shoulders were slumped, and tears were streaming down his face.

I had him pull himself out of the experience and become an observer from an adult perspective. This is a helpful way for someone to examine a painful moment and gain insight without having to be in the pain of it. By doing this, Gary was able to witness his young self, look into his eyes, and express compassion and love for that part of himself. He lovingly spoke the following to himself:

- "I love you."
- "You are smart and capable."
- "You are learning and growing every day."

I then instructed Gary to energetically ask his child self what he needed to believe in order to accept the words Gary spoke. He energetically felt that his young self needed gentle words, compassion, and hugs. Gary visualized his adult self holding his little boy self in his arms, stroking his hair, and sending loving energy to him.

Gary sat like this for some time, and when we completed the session, his posture was relaxed, and his voice was steady as he stated, "I can't believe how much better I feel."

It is essential for individuals to follow up on their healing experiences in hypnotherapy by engaging in activities or practices that help retain that healing. This is my reason for asking clients to do homework based on what they are working on.

Since Gary's child self had a desire for gentle words, compassion, and hugs, his assignment was to visualize holding his younger self daily. I instructed him to speak loving words to his child self while in visualization and to be aware of any intuitive thoughts and ideas that came up during this time.

During a process like this, our intuition can be activated, and ideas for additional ways to support can come up. Gary sensed that speaking the loving words aloud was very powerful. Our emotions are a magnet, and Gary was able to create a sense of loving compassion by visualizing holding his child self and speaking loving words aloud. This sense of loving energy was something he had never experienced before.

I also suggested that Gary do some journaling, specifically around the three phrases he told his child self while in hypnosis: "I love you," "You are smart and capable," and "You are learning and growing every day."

First, I instructed him to write each of those statements as an "I/ me" statement: "I love myself. I am smart and capable. I am learning and growing every day." As I mentioned in my chapter on affirmations, sometimes when we state something such as "I love myself" and don't feel it at all, it can have the opposite effect and remind us of all the ways we don't love ourselves. That's when I invite someone to say a willing or open statement such as "I am willing to love myself" or "I am open to loving myself." This helps open the door to the possibility of authentically feeling self-love.

When I requested that Gary rewrite the statements, he felt good saying, "I love you," and he also felt good saying, "I am learning and growing every day." However, "I am smart and capable" felt really challenging to him, so he changed that to "I am open to seeing myself as smart and capable." I asked Gary to write these statements and place them in prominent places in his home so that he would see them often.

I gave Gary one more writing assignment: to make a list of 50 loving activities he could do for himself. I told him he did not have to do all of the activities. I simply wanted him to come up with a robust list of possibilities and choose at least three each week to do. Shifting thoughts into self-love and what that looks like in one's life can have an impact on the things we do, on our self-talk, and even on how we allow others to treat us.

Gary had worked hard up to this point to open his heart and felt safe enough to really open up. He was ready for change and commit to the work. As I gave him his assignments, he was eager to begin, and I felt confident that he would follow through with his part. I was excited to see what would come next.

It was clear two weeks later when Gary walked into my office that things were beginning to shift for him. He stood a little taller, and his posture exuded a sense of confidence that I had not seen in him before.

As he sat down, he confirmed my initial reaction. "I can't believe how much better I feel in just two weeks! So many things have come to me." He continued excitedly, "A few days after starting the journaling and visualization, I realized that it was true. I am smart. Being a yoga instructor, and the organizational skills it takes to put a class together, require intelligence."

He also found that the trouble he generally experienced with technology was shifting. Rather than approaching the online scheduler and other work tasks with dread, he told himself, "I can do this. I am smart." He took his time, went step by step, and had much greater success.

Now that Gary had begun to feel better about himself and his professional abilities, he questioned the sustainability of his relationship with his girlfriend, Ellen. He knew he wanted something more but didn't know how to get it. "I get tired of all the arguing. I feel like she has no respect for me and puts me down," Gary complained. "She doesn't like the way I do the laundry or put away groceries. She's always complaining about something. It's like I can't do anything right." As he shared more about the relationship, it became clear that there were many similarities between the way his mother treated him and Ellen's behavior.

As I explained to Gary, we often seek relationships that, in some way, mirror our early relationships, even when those were unhappy or dysfunctional. We don't desire to repeat the relationship; we subconsciously seek comfort in the discomfort of the familiar. Things can look great to a casual observer, but beneath the surface is a pattern of dysfunction.

Growing up, Gary often found himself striving to prove himself to his mother by attempting to excel in areas that were not his natural strengths. He spent a great deal of time studying math and science, and no matter how much he tried, he simply wasn't the A student his mother wanted him to be. When he fell short of her expectations, he felt like a failure, and his mother reinforced those beliefs with her words, often declaring he was "stupid and would never amount to anything."

Ellen, in many ways, mirrored these traits. She was charming and deeply caring but also could be judgmental and condescending. She would often get upset and blame Gary over minor issues. She consistently corrected things like the way he loaded the dishwasher, did laundry, and managed finances. Gary resisted and became defensive when Ellen voiced these criticisms and, in a strange way, felt comforted in the familiarity.

"I know she cares about me and is trying to be helpful," he told me.

Although he hadn't consciously chosen a partner who behaved like his mother, the familiarity in the disapproval was a known script he could follow. Navigating the highs and lows with Ellen felt almost second nature because he had done it for so many years.

Despite the emotional exhaustion, Gary often felt a sense of purpose in trying to please Ellen. It subconsciously gave him a sense of control and belief that if he could please her, it meant that he wasn't stupid or incapable of being successful.

We began exploring the relationship using hypnosis to tap into his higher self, the part of him that goes beyond the ego and the conditioned "shoulds" that we adopt in life. I guided Gary, in a trance state, to imagine what his life would be like one year from now if he maintained his relationship with Ellen as it was. These are the words he spoke:

"I am distracted. I am focused on making her happy."

"Nothing I do is right. I am a failure."

"I can't do this. It's so hard."

His shoulders slumped forward, and he seemed to be sinking into the chair. His eyebrows were furrowed, his jaw was clenched, and his lips were pressed tightly together.

I then guided him to move from that image and experience what life would look like in a year if he ended the relationship. He stated the following:

"I feel lighter and free."

"I am more myself."

"I have time and energy for me and my career."

"I want more. I feel alone."

Gary's posture was upright, and his arms were loosely laid on his lap. His jaw had dropped slightly, and his eyebrows had relaxed.

As he mentioned feeling alone, I inquired whether he was lonely or alone. We can be alone and be completely content, or we can be alone and long to be with someone.

Gary clarified, "I long to be in a relationship with someone." As he spoke, his lips downturned, and his voice was quivering. I could feel his sadness.

"What do you believe about yourself in being alone?" I inquired.

"Nobody loves me," he said. "I am not good enough. I will be alone forever."

These were the beliefs I knew we had to work through in subsequent sessions. They were the ones that kept him in a relationship where he was judged and criticized.

In the following session, I asked Gary, while in a trance state, to visualize a shift in his relationship with Ellen. What would need to happen for him to feel valued and appreciated, and specifically, what was his part in it?

At first, it was all about her and what she said and did that was hurtful to him. I gently guided him to look at his behavior as well. How did he respond when she corrected him? Could he perhaps do something different?

This can be a slippery slope. I did not want to feed into his negative self-perception, but I did want him to see how he could improve and break the cycle. Rather than seeing Ellen as "the bad guy" and himself as "the victim," he could ask himself if she could potentially be right about some of the things she says.

It doesn't necessarily mean that she's right about everything. It is also possible that she's not wrong about everything. By working to release some of that victim energy, it is easier to look at a situation and ask, "What is my part?" Gary could then become empowered to make a shift and do his part to create the desired change in their relationship.

Of course, there are times when a relationship is abusive. Controlling behavior, extreme jealousy, isolation, and verbal abuse are all signs of an abusive relationship, and it is crucial to seek support if you are experiencing this.

In Gary's relationship, although Ellen was often critical, there were also times when she was very supportive, particularly in encouraging him with his work. She often praised his ability to teach yoga and was impressed with his knowledge. Also, Gary never felt unsafe or unable to walk away.

I reminded him that he is the only one he can change. Being in a relationship is much like doing a dance. One partner makes a move, and the other moves in response. If one partner changes the steps, the other must change too. We can't always predict what that change will be; however, change will occur.

Gary and Ellen were doing a dance. Ellen complained about Gary. Gary felt dejected and sad. She got mad when he didn't change, and he played the victim role, feeling sorry for himself, which made her the villain.

In a trance state, I had Gary go to a recent time when they had a disagreement about him "not doing something correctly." He recalled an exchange they had a few days earlier about loading the dishwasher. While this might seem minor, it is indeed indicative of the types of arguments they had, and the inquiry into possibilities to change the steps is similar for both minor and major issues.

As Gary spoke about the disagreement, he said things like, "She always complains," "She never appreciates what I do," and "Nothing I do is right."

I asked him to consider the possibility that she was correct. What if there was a better way to load the dishwasher? What if it was more efficient and effective?

Gary took a long pause. It had never occurred to him that she could have a valid point. As he considered some of the points she had made, he saw the validity in them. Mixing the types of silverware in the compartment let the water flow more easily, and food didn't get stuck. Having a system around the placement of the plates created more room, allowing the dishwasher to be run less frequently and saving energy.

Gary had been conditioned to become defensive when confronted with any criticism, even constructive criticism. He jumped to blaming the critic and taking on a victim role as opposed to being curious and considering a potential new way of doing things. This played out repeatedly in his relationship with his mother.

I guided him to think about other previous relationships where he felt unappreciated and severely criticized. As he touched on relationship after relationship—some intimate, some friendships—it was a clear pattern for him.

It is essential to clearly see that pattern in order to shift it. Gary believed that he wasn't valued and that people always found fault with him. Remember, when we have a belief, we unconsciously set out to prove it.

Gary's previous girlfriend complained about his driving, in particular his parking. Upon discussing, he confessed he actually did struggle to parallel park. A friend often complained that Gary was indecisive and rarely made suggestions for activities. Upon reflecting on that, he realized it was his lack of confidence that was causing him to stay quiet. Gary's newfound openness in sharing with his friend has significantly helped their friendship grow.

Once Gary saw the pattern, the next step was to explore ways to shift it. I deeply believe that we all have the answers within ourselves, and my work is to support people in accessing those answers.

As Gary leaned into his inner wisdom, it was clear that there was resistance to admitting to Ellen that she might be correct. He was deeply attached to his role as the victim and portraying Ellen as the villain.

"What if there is no victim or villain?" I asked him. "Can you imagine the gray area in the middle? Perhaps you are partially correct and not 100% correct."

Gary sat in silence for a few moments. "I never really considered that."

A teacher of mine has said, "Pain pushes until vision pulls." Gary's pain pushed him toward victim defensiveness. A clear vision of the kind of relationship he desired could instead pull him toward releasing the resistance and embracing curiosity.

While in hypnosis, Gary visualized the ideal relationship. He wanted kindness, communication, laughter, respect, and freedom to be himself. The question then became: Who does he need to be, and how does he need to show up in that relationship? He envisioned himself smiling and laughing more. He also saw himself actively listening to Ellen and being curious rather than shutting down when she started complaining or correcting him.

Over the next several months, he worked on just that—pausing before reacting, considering how he would want to be treated, communicating his desires, and actively listening to Ellen. When she complained about the way he loaded the dishwasher, he was able to let his defenses down and really hear what she was saying. He stopped taking things so seriously, and they both experienced more joy and laughter—even laughing about the dishwasher loading they had argued so much about in the past. He also spent a good deal of time by himself, getting to know what honestly mattered to him. He found that he really enjoyed meditation and now has a dedicated daily practice. This has helped him learn to pause and be more curious when he feels judged.

All of this is not to say it was easy and without bumps in the road. True change takes time and consistent effort. Gary put in time and effort with affirmations, visualization, and meditation and is now reaping the rewards in the form of a happy, mutually satisfying relationship. In the process, Ellen noticed some behaviors in herself that she wanted to further explore. She realized that she was quick to criticize and slow to praise. She was also very rigid about household chores and how they should be done. She is now seeing a therapist and learning to understand what drives these tendencies.

I am happy to report that their communication has vastly improved, and they are both committed to bringing their best to the relationship. Through Heart Shift, Gary rewrote his victim story and is more confident and secure in who he is.

The guided process I used with Gary to connect him to the loving energy within his heart is included in the book portal for your reference.

Journal prompt

Reflect upon a time in your life when you received criticism.

- If you were to observe your behavior or actions from an unbiased perspective, in what ways might the critiques hold true or provide insights for growth?

Chapter 16

Heart Shift Using Affirmations and Visioning

Marin's Story

MARIN SHOWED UP at my office completely dejected and down on everything, especially men. As she stepped into my office, I noticed her eyes were teary and her expression flat.

"I just got passed over for the third time for the role of executive chef," she said as the tears flowed down her cheeks. "I have spent the last five years working myself ragged, and I know I am a good chef. I'm one of the reasons they're a top restaurant here in Chicago," she continued, her voice rising in anger. "They only promote the male chefs," she said, crossing her arms and leaning back against the couch.

She is a hard worker and dedicated to her craft. She works long hours, including every weekend. She spends her off time creating new recipes and perfecting them. Food is her passion and has been since she was a child. Unfortunately, the role of executive chef in the restaurant industry is heavily dominated by men. According to *Forbes*, women occupy only 6.3% of the head chef positions at prominent U.S. restaurant groups.

"I have dreamt of opening my own restaurant for as long as I can remember. I would serve eclectic cuisine with women running the kitchen," she said with a glimmer of excitement.

"What is stopping you from doing just that?" I asked.

"I have a huge student loan and credit card debt," she explained. "I haven't been able to cover my basic living expenses with my current salary. I never have enough money. My family doesn't support me at all! I am destined to work myself to the bone for someone else to gain the glory," she said.

Part of her felt completely hopeless, yet she showed up at my office that day and asked for help. Supporting her in getting in touch with her higher why by creating a vision for what she wanted to create was essential. However, her Lack Consciousness, which circled around being a woman in a male-dominated field, was the first obstacle to tackle. As Henry Ford famously said, "Whether you think you can, or you think you can't—you're right." Marin's consciousness was filled with lack thoughts around money and opportunity. This needed to shift to possibility before anything could change.

For me, this hit close to home. My husband and I experienced a challenging period financially about 12 years ago. We lost a lot, including making the tough decision to sell our home and downsize before we ever thought we would. While there was much heartache and sadness surrounding that decision, I learned and grew a lot. Over time, I released my attachment to "things" and became much more focused on the experience of life and the quality of relationships. I also deepened my faith in the universe and noticed that, despite the loss, I had so much to be grateful for—primarily my husband, children, and mother. Putting those relationships first, including an amazing circle of close friends, made all the difference in how I moved through that experience.

One of the key lessons I learned was that Lack Consciousness versus Abundance Consciousness has nothing to do with how much money you have. Lack Consciousness is a belief that, regardless of how much money you have, it is a finite amount, and there is often fear around losing it, someone taking it, or it simply not being enough.

Abundance Consciousness, on the other hand, is faith and trust that whatever you have, there is more available to you, and it is not finite. We could get fired, a company could shut down, or something else could happen that would make it impossible to get paid. When we have the belief that we can weather the storm and find our way to being sourced by another means, we have Abundance Consciousness. This is true freedom.

As I was experiencing a lot of loss, I was terrified as I watched the bank account dwindle with no money coming in. As often happens in moments like that, I had no choice but to surrender and turn to my faith in a higher power. I practiced meditation, affirmative prayer, and read every abundance book I could get my hands on. I realized the ways I contributed to things getting out of hand—primarily, turning my back on what I didn't want to see and failing to have a safety net of emergency savings. It was this experience that caused me to gain control over my finances and spending in a way I had never done before. It wasn't easy, and I wouldn't wish it on anyone. It was a wake-up call for me and is now a way I can support others.

Marin shared that she grew up in a middle-class neighborhood, and both her parents worked for large companies. She was an only child, and when she told her parents she wanted to go to culinary school rather than a four-year college, they were against it.

"You won't be able to support yourself. The restaurant business is unstable," they said. They refused to help her pay for school, although they had the means to do so.

She went ahead and proceeded with her plan despite their disappointment. She excelled at school and loved every minute of it. The financial challenge for her came when she had to start repaying the student loan, and she was barely making above minimum wage. She got herself into significant credit card debt—not because she was extravagant, but because she couldn't make ends meet on what she was earning at the restaurant.

In hypnosis, Marin expressed her desire to be financially free. She felt that until she paid off her credit card debt, she didn't deserve anything good. She stated, "I am a no-good slacker."

Knowing that she was a very hard and dedicated worker, I asked, "Whose voice is saying you're a no-good slacker?"

She paused and said, "My mom." Tears began streaming down her face, and her shoulders rounded. I asked her if it was true, and she said, "No. I work really, really hard, but I still don't make any progress paying off my credit cards. It's hopeless."

I explained that having that voice in her head was part of what was keeping her from making progress.

"Do you want to let go of that voice?" I asked.

"Yes."

"Tell your mother now, out loud, that it is not true, you don't believe it, and it must stop now."

"Stop now," she said. "I work hard. I deserve to be happy."

There is great power in the spoken word. Stating something like that, especially in a trance state, makes a huge impression on the subconscious mind. As Marin spoke those words with conviction, I witnessed her begin to sit up taller and pull back her shoulders. It was clear that she was feeling the words.

I sensed that was not the only voice in Marin's head. Her assignment after that session was to pay attention to the negative self-talk and speak gentle, loving affirmations to herself.

Whenever we have negative self-talk or thoughts, it is necessary to not give them more energy or attention than they already have. We cannot change what we are unaware of, so the first step in shifting unwanted behaviors is noticing them. Then, we can gently speak kind and loving words to ourselves, replacing the negative thought with something positive that we want to embrace.

In Marin's case, I suggested noticing the negative thought and then saying something like, "I am not interested in that thought" or "That is not my truth," followed by something like, "I am actually a dedicated, hard-working employee" or "I deserve success in every area of my life."

When Marin stepped into my office the following week, I noticed she held her head up high and made direct eye contact. It was clear that a shift was beginning; however, there was still more work to be done. To make lasting change, it is necessary to uncover limiting beliefs and shift them.

Marin recalled that from a young age, her parents had instilled in her the belief that the way to get ahead and support yourself was to find a good company to work for, stick with that company, get your retirement, and live a modest life. But Marin knew that was not her path.

When she was in the kitchen, she became alive and animated. It started with her play kitchen and toy food at a young age, and once she was able to experiment in the real kitchen at age eight, she radiated joy. She experimented with various flavors, seasonings, and ingredients. She knew that was where she belonged.

While Marin was on her journey to becoming an excellent chef, her parents continuously opposed her, reiterating that she was headed down the wrong path. Fortunately, Marin had the support of friends and colleagues who saw what she was capable of, and they continued to encourage her. Even with this encouragement, Marin still struggled with doubts and the belief that she would never really be able to support herself and live a comfortable life.

Our work together was to dig into those beliefs that were holding her back and erase them from her consciousness. As Marin went into a trance state that day, she recalled a time when she was about five years old. She was creating a meal using toy food in her play kitchen, excited about her creations. She made unique food combinations and names for her dishes. When she showed them to her parents and grandmother, they laughed.

Something in Marin, even at that young age, was hurt by that laughter. As we explored this further, she recalled feeling that something was wrong with her.

While Marin continued to sit in her trance state, we progressed to when she was around eight or nine years old, making food in the real kitchen. She told her mother that she couldn't wait to be a grown-up and cook in a restaurant. Her mother laughed and said, "That's no career for a woman, and you won't make any money. Maybe you'll be a teacher. That is a respectable profession."

As a result of this conversation, Marin believed that being a cook or chef was not only not respectable but that she wouldn't be able to support herself. Sadly, it became a self-fulfilling prophecy. Years later, Marin struggled to make ends meet and relied on her credit cards to fill in the gaps. She believed that she could not adequately support herself doing what she loved.

As we continued to work on shifting this belief, we went back to the source. While she was in a trance state, I instructed Marin, "Go back to the source of your belief that you can't support yourself doing what you love." It turned out that when she was around six or seven, she overheard an argument between her parents about money.

Dad: "I'm miserable at the office. I'm not respected, and I'm undervalued."

Mom: "You have to keep going. We have bills to pay, and my salary can't possibly cover them. We have to take care of Marin."

Dad: "I know that you're right, but I'm so unhappy."

Mom: "I'm sorry. It's the only way to survive."

Marin took these words to heart. She stated that her belief was, *You can't support yourself and be happy—it's one or the other.* Her current experience proved this to be true.

It was essential for Marin to see that this belief was not absolute truth. Understanding and feeling this while in a trance would magnify the experience and support her in creating a new belief.

I first asked her, "Do you know if this is absolutely the truth? Is there anyone on this planet who is doing something they love, supporting themselves, and even thriving in that work?"

Her response was, "Yes, but…" She had all the excuses. "That's not me. Success is for other people. Men have it easier in the restaurant industry," and so on.

I reminded Marin of the power of belief and its impact on achieving one's goals. Take Roger Bannister, for instance. He shattered the belief that running a mile in under four minutes was impossible by clocking in at three minutes and 59 seconds. What's amazing is that just 46 days after breaking the record, another runner surpassed his time. This proves that when we see someone accomplishing what was once believed to be impossible, it creates a sense of possibility in others. I urged Marin to consider the countless individuals who pursue their passions and find joy and success in them.

Marin's assignment for the next week was to do some research and find people having success doing what they love. I asked her to seek out a variety of people—those with huge success, those with moderate success, and those in between. Whether they were people she knew or people she'd read about, the idea was to get immersed in possibility. We had already begun this by planting the suggestion while in a trance state, and this assignment was meant to reinforce that work.

When Marin came to my office the following week, she was bubbling with excitement over what she had learned. She had many examples of people finding success doing what they loved and this renewed her enthusiasm for her work. Among the examples were several female chefs in the Midwest, including:

- **Stephanie Izard** – Based in Chicago and known for winning *Top Chef,* Stephanie is also the owner and chef of Girl & the Goat, Little Goat, and Duck Duck Goat.
- **Ann Kim** – The owner and chef of Young Joni, Pizzeria Lola, and Hello Pizza in Minneapolis. She is known for her creative and gourmet take on pizzas, and Young Joni has received national acclaim.
- **Liz Valenti** – The head chef and co-owner of Wheat Penny Oven and Bar in Dayton, Ohio. Her work emphasizes innovative pizzas and a farm-to-table approach that highlights local produce.

Marin's next step was to begin shifting her beliefs about money beyond career, work, and earnings. This is a reciprocal universe—what we give out, we receive, whether it's kindness, a gift, or even a simple, nice word. I often find that when people are financially struggling, the issue is that their ability to receive is out of balance. When we become more open to receiving in different areas of life, we create an energy of receptivity, which can ultimately lead to greater financial abundance.

In my personal experience, I noticed during our financially challenging time that I am very much a giver—giving of my time, my energy, and whatever someone might need. I was always the first one to volunteer for something, whether it was at my kids' school, within the family, or at the spiritual center.

I realized that I was out of balance with giving and receiving. While being a generous, giving person feels good and is not something I wanted to stop, I didn't allow others to give to me. My response to someone offering a helping hand was, "Oh no, I can take care of that," or "I don't need help." When, in fact, having a helping hand would have felt supportive and loving.

When I first started making a shift in this area, it felt uncomfortable. I found myself saying no to things that I normally would have said yes to, and I found myself saying yes to offers of support and help. For example, someone offered to co-chair a committee I was on. How wonderful it was not to have all the responsibility! It took some time, but eventually, I was able to accept help, do a little less, and feel good about it.

In working with Marin, I realized that she was also out of balance in the areas of giving and receiving in her life, so that is where our work continued.

I did a process with Marin, tapping into the energy of her inner child. Rather than recalling a specific memory or event, it was more of a symbolic journey. I guided her to enter a room that would shed light on her current state of Lack Consciousness. She entered a room that was much like an altar in a religious building. There were beautiful, ornate objects on the altar, and she was very small; she could not reach, touch, or have any of them.

"Tell me what you see," I said.

"Beautiful golden candelabras and chalices."

"Are they yours?"

"No. I can't touch them. They're not for me."

"Tell me more about that."

"I'm not big enough," she said. "I don't know how to get to them. I really don't deserve them anyway."

I noticed that Marin was slouched, her lips were turned downward, and tears were rolling down her cheeks.

"Do you want these things?"

"Yes, they're beautiful."

"When did you start to believe you don't deserve these things?"

"Beautiful things and riches are for other people. Rich people have those things. They are smarter."

As Marin spoke about "rich people," I noticed a look of disdain on her face. Her features sort of crunched up, and she pulled back a little bit. It was clear that she had a strong opinion about rich people, which was not positive.

Many people facing financial challenges may feel resentful toward those with wealth. Sometimes, this can be interpreted as jealousy, but it's imperative to consider the deeper emotions at play. Our mindset and energy play a crucial role in how we approach life. If we harbor negative feelings toward a certain group, like those with money, we might unintentionally drive away opportunities for prosperity in our own lives.

It's essential to remember that, just as with any group, people with wealth come in all personalities—from the exceptionally kind and generous to the selfish and greedy. Generalizations about any group, including those with abundant resources, aren't constructive. Instead, realizing that there are many good and generous people who have money creates positive energy around wealth, making us more energetically able to attract it for ourselves.

As Marin and I discussed this, she became aware of how often she had heard negative things about wealthy people throughout her childhood. Her parents were resentful of neighbors and acquaintances whom they saw as well-off and not needing to work hard. They often said things like,

"Those people are lazy. They got everything handed to them,"

or

"They must have cheated somehow and not paid their taxes."

Marin formed the opinion that they were all selfish and that they must have done something dishonest to acquire all that money—or it had been handed to them from previous generations. While this may be true for some, it is not true for all. Although some are born into wealth, that doesn't necessarily mean they don't work to preserve and grow their wealth. It also doesn't mean they don't do good with the resources they have. She never really considered that people could work, dedicate themselves to doing work they loved, and actually make money.

While Marin understood intellectually that not all rich people were selfish, in her gut, she wasn't sure. The ingrained beliefs we hold can be very strong. In order to acknowledge those beliefs and see more clearly that they were false, I asked Marin to simply notice how often negative thoughts about rich people came up in her mind and, when they did, to say to herself, *"And I am willing to change my belief about that person."* She could then imagine, based on whatever her thought was, how the opposite might be true.

For example, if the thought was, *"Look at that person with all that expensive jewelry! What a waste of money. There are people who could use that money to feed their children,"* she would need to shift that thought. While there are certainly people struggling to feed their children, Marin couldn't know if this person did or did not make contributions to others. Also, the designers of that jewelry may be artists creating and doing work they love.

By approaching others with understanding, we might see that everyone's choices—especially about how they spend their money—stem from their own experiences and perspectives. We only catch a glimpse of their journey. By focusing on the goodness in others, we often inspire that goodness to shine even brighter.

After all, isn't our deepest wish to uplift one another? By framing our thoughts and actions with positivity, we not only radiate acceptance and love but also draw this very energy to ourselves.

After working on this for several months, Marin became more accepting of others and began to look for the best in people—not only in those with wealth but in others as well. Recently, she met her cousin's new girlfriend, who comes from a wealthy family. Instead of going into that introduction with a preconceived belief that she was selfish or spoiled in some way, Marin chose to approach it with the expectation that she was a kind and caring person, and that is exactly what she discovered. She also found herself smiling more and being friendlier with cashiers and others she encountered. People overwhelmingly reacted in a pleasant and kind manner. It was beginning to become a habit. Like developing any habit, the process requires time and dedication. It was Marin's commitment to realizing her dream that fueled her dedication to sticking with it.

One relationship in particular that improved was with the chef who received the promotion she wanted. Marin had held a good deal of resentment toward him. As she became more introspective, she was able to see that while she had felt more qualified and had been there longer, it wasn't his fault that the owner chose him for the promotion. He worked hard and was very good at what he did.

As she began respecting him more, she actually learned some new techniques from him, and he consulted her when making menu changes. They developed a good working relationship based on mutual respect. While she had always felt joy in the kitchen doing her work, she now felt even more comfortable at the restaurant working with this particular chef.

Now that Marin was feeling more financially hopeful and comfortable with the promoted chef, it seemed like a good time to begin looking to the future and creating a vision for what she wanted in her life. Having a vision and creating intentions and goals around it supports us in achieving our dreams. Without clear goals and a plan to reach them, it is hard to move forward. As Benjamin Franklin said, "If you fail to plan, you plan to fail."

Visioning, as I explained earlier, is about catching that higher plan for your life. During visioning, we're in a meditative state, tuning into that inner higher wisdom. Marin and I visioned several times over the next month, and a couple of themes came up. One was a desire for clarity and security, and the other was opening her own restaurant.

Up to this point, Marin did not have a plan for paying off her credit card debt or student loans. She let her mail go unopened for weeks at a time because she simply did not want to face it. Her credit score was low because she often made payments late. Her dream of opening her own restaurant, while still alive within her, felt impossible.

The good news is that with the other changes she was making—viewing people with wealth in a more positive light and the renewed hope that she could also live her dream—she was feeling optimistic. She had a desire and excitement about creating a plan for herself.

One of the classes I taught at the spiritual center was called Financial Freedom. I use several of the tools from this class with my clients. The two pillars that are the basis for the class are order and balance. Creating order is about knowing where you stand, having a plan, and following through with it. Creating balance is simply not spending more than you bring in.

Marin agreed that her top priority was sorting through the mail to gain a clear picture of her financial situation. We did a hypnotherapy session to address what was blocking her from doing this. What came up was a fear that if she looked at it and saw what she actually owed, there would be no way to pay it down, and it would be too overwhelming.

During the session, I guided Marin to a time when she overcame an obstacle that felt insurmountable.

"Culinary school was really tough," she shared. "I barely had any money to live on, and the student loans were paying for school. I worked really hard and excelled in my classes," she said with a smile. "I was really proud of how I handled that. I felt so strong and powerful."

"Now allow yourself to use that same energy that got you through school as you think about opening the mail, writing everything down, and creating order. Imagine what it will feel like to not only know where you stand but have a plan to move forward and realize your dream. Order is the first step, and you have the strength and will to create that order. Allow yourself to feel it at the core of your being," I said.

As she visualized this, I saw her sit up taller and straighter.

"I can do this. I am strong. I have the power to do hard things," she confidently stated.

I could hear the conviction in her words.

The next time Marin walked into my office, there was confidence in her stride and a smile on her face. "I opened up all the mail, listed the amounts I owe, and it was less than I thought!" she exclaimed. "I'm experiencing a newfound sense of clarity and freedom."

Her next step was to create a repayment plan. We discussed options, including bankruptcy, a loan, and calls to creditors to set up payment plans. After considering various options, I guided Marin to get in touch with her higher self, and we tested out each scenario, observing how she felt in her body. Marin settled on calling the creditors to set up payment plans and closing accounts so she would not continue to accrue interest. While she did feel some fear around this, she knew in her heart and gut that this was the right choice.

This was almost a year ago, and Marin has been steadily and regularly paying her debt. What she has noticed is the freedom she feels and the satisfaction of seeing the amount she owes decrease rather than increase. When she really examined her expenses, she found ways to cut down and started working a few more hours a week to bring in additional income. She is well on her way and expects to be debt-free in a few months!

I also encouraged Marin to create a spending plan for herself. As the name suggests, it focuses on how and where she wants to spend her money. I prefer the term *spending plan* over *budget*, as the latter feels constricting and limiting, whereas *spending* feels more expansive. Marin's spending plan includes a small amount of savings each month for the restaurant she dreams of opening. As she pays off her debt, that amount will continue to grow.

In addition to the spending plan, Marin created a vision board for her restaurant. One day, she walked into my office with the vision board, proudly showing me every image and describing what it meant to her.

"Every time I look at this, I feel hopeful, excited, and exhilarated," she said. The board was filled with images of food, kitchens, and people laughing and talking while dining. "The most amazing part is that I actually feel it's possible," she added. "As much as I have always envisioned this, I don't think I ever really believed I could have it. Now I believe it with my whole heart."

We continued discussing how everything was going. "Even the spending plan is working!" she exclaimed. "Documenting my progress makes it feel real, and even small changes in my spending are adding up!"

Marin shifted her deep-seated scarcity mindset into an abundance mindset by using affirmations and visioning. She also brought order and balance to her finances, giving her a sense of stability. Marin's Heart Shift has enabled her to move closer to her dream of opening her own restaurant. She enthusiastically believes it will happen, and she is well on her way!

Journal prompt

Reflect on the nature of your consciousness.

- Do you find that it leans more toward a sense of scarcity or abundance?

Examine your readiness to accept and receive.

- Are you open to the gifts that life has to offer you?

Chapter 17

Heart Shift Using Meditation and Self-Love

Annie's Story

"I CAN'T LIVE LIKE this any longer," Annie exclaimed as she plopped down on the couch in my office. "Every time I start having hope, it starts up again," she sobbed, reaching for the tissues.

"What's going on?" I asked, wondering what could be causing this desperation.

"It's been going on literally for years," she said, almost shouting.

I had never seen Annie before and could sense that she was so focused on whatever was happening that she was not fully present. I instructed her to place her feet flat on the floor, uncross her arms, and focus on her body being supported by the couch she was sitting on while consciously trying to slow her breath.

"Inhale as I count—one, two, three. Hold—one, two, three, four. Now exhale—one, two, three, four, five."

After a few rounds of breathing in this way, I sensed she was more grounded.

"Can you tell me about what you are experiencing?"

"There's something wrong with my stomach. I have been to five different doctors and had all kinds of tests, and they can't find anything wrong! They say it is all in my head," she said with disgust. "I know I am not crazy, and I know how I feel," she asserted.

"Of course, you know how you feel. Tell me what you are experiencing," I replied.

"I get really nauseous at random times for no reason," she shared.

I explained to Annie that our bodies are always talking to us, and we should learn how to listen. While it is absolutely vital to get our symptoms checked out by a doctor, it is also necessary to uncover any underlying emotional cause for pain and/or disease.

"I would like to help you connect to your stomach through hypnosis to see what is causing the nausea," I said. I knew from our conversation prior to her session that she had never experienced hypnosis before and was open to it.

"Are you ready?" I inquired.

"Yes, please," she said.

"Get in a comfortable position and gently close your eyes as you begin to focus on your breath. Allow yourself to lean into the rhythmic nature of the breath," I said, continuing to guide her into a trance state.

My objective for this first session was to gauge her responsiveness to hypnosis and make sure she felt comfortable while hopefully providing some relief. Annie entered the trance state relatively quickly. I guided her to connect with her heart and all the loving energy within her heart. She had already let me know that she had a strong faith in God. Her belief was that God is within and is all good. I reminded her that God was right there with her in her heart.

As we proceeded in the session, I instructed her to send loving energy to her stomach.

"Imagine all the loving energy in your heart pouring down upon your stomach. Feel the warmth and comfort of it as it fills and surrounds your stomach."

As I continued, I told her to say words of gratitude to her stomach for all that it does for her.

"Thank you for digesting the food I eat. I am grateful for the way you support the nourishment of my body and let me know when I need more or have had enough."

As she spoke, her furrowed brows began to relax, her jaw dropped a bit, and her whole face began to soften.

"And what does your stomach need from you?" I asked.

There was a long pause as her breath became deeper and more even. When she spoke, her voice was slow and deliberate.

"It wants me to relax and calm down, to stop creating pressure." Her tone was almost a whisper.

"How does it want you to do that?" I inquired.

Another long pause.

"Breathe fully and deeply. Be happy," she said, her words tinged with hope.

As I brought Annie out of the trance state and back into the room, she appeared much more relaxed and calm. Her face was softer, and her shoulders were less tense.

Her first question was, "How am I supposed to be happy when I get nauseous all the time?" Her voice quivered slightly with a trace of frustration.

"Perhaps the first step is, as you said, to breathe fully and deeply," I responded.

And that was Annie's homework for the first week. I instructed her to set aside a few minutes, several times a day, to simply practice breathing. Additionally, when she felt nauseous, she was to breathe fully and deeply, allowing the rhythm of her breath to anchor her, easing the discomfort.

When Annie returned to my office the following week, there was a slight decrease in her level of agitation. However, I could still sense her impatience and anxiousness.

"The whole breathing thing does feel good, but I'm still getting nauseous," she admitted. Her voice was mixed with resignation and a bit of relief.

I wasn't surprised that she was still experiencing nausea, as we hadn't really gotten into any root cause at this point. My goal for this session was to go deeper into hypnosis to uncover the cause of her nausea.

"Let's see if we can get to the source of this nausea. Are you ready for hypnosis?" I asked.

"Yes, please," she eagerly declared.

While she was in a trance, it became clear that Annie had a lot of worry and anxiety. She worried about her stomach issues due to the nausea, which was understandable. However, she also had many more irrational worries that caused her to spiral into a state of panic.

For example, she was afraid of getting trapped in an elevator. The building where she worked as a sales representative required her to ride the elevator daily, as did many of the offices she regularly visited.

"Every time I get in, my heart races, and I pray the doors will open and I won't plunge to my death," she said tearfully.

She was also haunted by the fear of contracting some obscure fatal illness. The fact that she had undiagnosed nausea exacerbated this fear.

As the fears came up during hypnosis, I asked, "Where in your body do you feel the fear?"

"It's in my stomach."

"What is the physical feeling?"

"Like I'm going to throw up."

"Is it a familiar feeling?"

"Yes!"

I then guided her back to the source—the first time she felt the feeling.

"I was really little, two or three, I think. My mom was taking me somewhere, and she was afraid. She didn't want to get in the elevator, but she had to. I was in my stroller."

"Why did you believe she was afraid?"

"She wasn't smiling, and she wasn't paying attention to me. I felt scared. Something was wrong, and I didn't know what."

"What happened next?"

"We got in the elevator, and her whole face changed and got scrunched up. It was so scary."

As she spoke, I noticed her jaw clench, her forehead crease, and she seemed to be shrinking into the couch.

"Tell me what you came to believe about yourself and life as a result of this experience."

"Life is scary. Elevators are scary. I am not safe," she said, lips trembling.

"How did your behavior change as a result of these beliefs?"

"I don't trust elevators. I don't trust anything I don't have control over," she replied.

We then explored how these beliefs and behaviors had impacted her life. While getting in an elevator is something she does on a regular basis, it is not easy, and she often feels sick when doing so. At one point, she was so terrified that she declined a job offer because she would not only have to ride an elevator to her office, but also several times a day between floors because the company had space on several floors. As a young girl, she looked at her mother's reaction to gauge whether she was safe. She often saw fear and worry in her mother and took that on. This inherited anxiety became woven into the fabric of her being.

Although I sensed the anxiety and worry went beyond elevators, I felt that releasing some of that fear would support the deeper work.

Annie's assignment for the next week was to research elevator safety. I also guided her to practice meditation daily using the breathing technique I had shown her to help her reach a meditative state. Having a regular meditation practice can provide the muscle memory to easily enter a relaxed state.

While Annie's research into elevator safety was helpful intellectually, there was still a good deal of anxiety when she stepped into the elevator. To further the progress, I used a titration process in hypnosis to demonstrate that, although she did not have true control over the elevator, she did have control over her reaction.

In hypnotherapy, titration involves guiding the client to gradually modify their response to a challenging experience. By allowing the client, while in trance, to experience something challenging and then guiding them to a state of calm, they can see a way out. As this is repeated, the client learns to calm and bring themselves out of panic and worry in the situation. This can sometimes happen in one session, and it can often take several sessions. The key is to go slow and be gentle so as not to create any additional trauma.

Since Annie's experience was that she picked up on her mother's fear, I suspected that getting her to step into her power and calm herself would work for her.

Once she was in a trance state, I guided her to her most calm and relaxing place. For her, it was the forest preserve near where she grew up. As a young girl, she loved walking the trail and exploring nature. "Use all your senses to be in that forest preserve right now."

Her facial muscles relaxed, and she looked so peaceful as she stated, "I feel a gentle breeze, and the aroma of the trees and other plants is so strong."

"Tell me what you see."

"It's fall, my favorite time of the year, so there are leaves on the trail, and the colors are magnificent!"

"How are you feeling?"

"So calm, so relaxed, so happy," she said, smiling.

"I'd like you to place the tips of your thumb and forefinger of your dominant hand together. Allow this to be an anchor and to remind you of how you feel right now," I instructed.

After remaining in this position for a few minutes, I had her release her thumb and forefinger. "Let the image go completely. Now, begin to see, sense, and feel yourself stepping onto an elevator." Within a few moments, I saw her facial expression shift. Her brows furrowed, her lips pursed, and her shoulders stiffened.

"Tell me what you're feeling now."

"I don't want to get in that elevator. What if it gets stuck? What if it has a sudden drop?"

"How do you feel?"

"Terrified. I feel like throwing up."

"Place your thumb and forefinger together and take yourself to your favorite, most relaxing place—that beautiful forest preserve. Feel the warmth, see the beautiful colors of the leaves, hear them crackling under your feet as you walk down the path."

As I spoke, her face began to soften, her shoulders dropped a bit, and I could tell she was beginning to feel calm. I continued reminding her of all the things she spoke about at the forest preserve, and within a couple of minutes, she was back to being completely relaxed.

I repeated this process several times, and each time she returned to that state of calm more quickly. I then began giving less coaching around what she was seeing when she put her thumb and forefinger together, and she was doing more of it herself. Finally, I brought her to the state of anxiety around the elevator and told her to calm herself. She managed to do so quite efficiently.

Annie's homework was to use the finger position during her meditation to take herself to the forest preserve. This would support her in being able to use this tool during times of stress.

At her next session, she excitedly exclaimed, "I can't believe how much easier it is to get on the elevator. It has not caused me a stomachache all week!"

While this was good progress, I knew we had more work to do. Annie had several other primarily irrational fears, and while this could help with them, I felt she needed something more. Her first response to just about anything new was hesitation and fear.

Annie shared that her mom needed to be in control as much as possible and was pretty much afraid of everything. Swimming is dangerous; there are sharks in the ocean; there is a risk of drowning in a pool. Germs are everywhere—don't touch anything—you could get sick and die! COVID really supported this one for her. And the list goes on. Somewhere, at the core of Annie's being, she accepted many of these fears and the tendency to lead with fear when approaching something new.

In hypnosis, I guided Annie to the source of her stomachaches and the first time she experienced them.

Her voice quivered as she recounted, "I was in middle school, and I was super nervous about a presentation. I woke up with a terrible stomachache."

I leaned forward, gently speaking, "Energetically connect with your stomach now. Send it some loving energy. What is it trying to tell you?" I probed.

She shuddered. "It's not safe to give a presentation. Kids might laugh and make fun of me. I can't trust the teacher to protect me."

"What happens if the kids laugh and make fun?"

"I will be embarrassed, humiliated. They will know that I don't know what I am doing."

"Then what happens?" I encouraged her to continue.

"I won't have any friends, and I'll be alone," she whispered.

"And if you're alone?"

"I'm a pathetic loser."

"If you are alone and a pathetic loser, what does that say about you?"

"Nobody loves me. I am unlovable. I will be alone forever."

Annie was slouched on the couch, withdrawn, and clearly, she was deeply sad.

"When you believe 'Nobody loves me. I am unlovable. I will be alone forever,' is that your belief or someone else's?"

Annie took a long pause. In a barely audible voice, she said, "It's my mom's."

"Tell me more," I encouraged softly, sensing the layers unfolding.

"She always had to control everything and have it perfect. If it wasn't, she was anxious and couldn't relax."

"Go on."

"One time when she was preparing for a dinner party, one of the dishes she made did not turn out well. She said things like, 'No one will want to come here again. I will be the laughingstock. I may as well give up now.' It sounds so intense, but that's the way she was. If it wasn't perfect, it was a disaster."

"And how do you react when things don't go as planned?" I asked, guiding her to connect the dots.

A look of comprehension came over Annie's face. "When things don't go well, or I lose control, I berate myself."

"Tell me what that looks like."

"I tell myself I'm stupid. Nothing I do is enough. People can see how flawed I am."

"Is that true?"

"No."

"What is true?"

"I always try my best. I get some things right."

At this point, I knew that the best way to combat the negative self-talk was through practicing self-love, kindness, and appreciation. I brought Annie out of the trance state and assigned the following homework:

- Make a list of your successes, focusing not on perfection but on things that went well.
- List your favorite qualities about yourself. Perhaps ask a friend for assistance to gain perspective.
- Notice when negative self-talk starts and immediately challenge the thought by asking questions such as: "Is this really true?" or "If I made a mistake, can I accept that I am human?"

At our next session, Annie had completed the homework, although she said it wasn't easy. She felt good when reflecting on her successes, one of which was learning to calm her fear of elevators.

The next step in our work was to connect with her younger self, the one who first took on the belief that she would be all alone if she made a mistake or wasn't perfect.

I guided Annie to a recent time when she felt pressure to be perfect. It was a sales presentation she was giving to a potential client.

"I was so nervous. I didn't sleep well the night before; my hands were clammy, and I was afraid my nerves would show. My stomach wasn't feeling great either," she shared.

I then counted back to take her to the first time she experienced that kind of anxiousness. She recalled a time at school when she had to give an oral book report at the age of nine.

"My hands were shaking, my palms sweaty, and my voice was quivering. It was awful!"

"What emotions were you experiencing?"

"Fear, anxiety—I wanted to run away."

"Where do you feel it?"

"My stomach. I'm nauseous."

As I guided Annie to connect to her stomach and give it a voice, the words emerged. "You don't know what you are talking about. You are stupid. The kids are going to laugh. You will not have any friends," she said as tears rolled down her cheeks and her hands trembled.

I then directed her to envision her nine-year-old self standing before her and tell that girl, "I love you, and you are not alone," I instructed softly. I asked Annie to gaze deeply into the child's eyes and notice what she saw.

"She's so lonely. Mom is so wrapped up in her own stuff, being perfect and all, she doesn't have time for her," Annie whispered.

"Ask her what she needs from you to feel loved and seen," I prompted.

"She wants kind words and more time to play," she said, her voice a mix of realization and sadness.

"What does more time to play look like?" I probed further.

"Being out in nature. Being spontaneous. More rest."

"Is that something you feel you can do?" I gently inquired.

"Yes." Annie nodded her head affirmatively.

"Let her know that you love her, you heard her, and you will do as she asked."

Annie did so, and once out of trance, we made a plan. The key component when doing the things her nine-year-old self desired is to do them consciously. Annie's homework was to connect with her child self during meditation, check in and see how she was doing, and intentionally get more rest, get outside, and allow time in her schedule for spontaneity.

At her next session, she was already starting to feel better. She was dealing with the control issues and anxiety on two levels-going to her favorite place when anxious, and building a strong foundation of self-love through connecting with her child self.

Over the course of the next several weeks, Annie developed habits from these practices, and she is reaping the benefits in the form of peace and calm. Through practicing meditation and self-love, she created her experience of Heart Shift.

Journal prompt

Reflect on things that worry you.

- Do you ever feel physical symptoms when worried?
- What insights from Annie's story might support you?

Conclusion

My greatest hope is that this book sheds light on the tools available to inspire you to create a Heart Shift and live your most empowered, healthy, and balanced life. The pillars I wrote about in Chapters Three through Nine outline some techniques you can use as you begin or continue on your journey.

- **Visioning & intention setting:** Clarify your desire and then take inspired action to manifest it.
- **Forgiveness:** Free yourself from the bondage of unforgiveness by following the steps provided.
- **Trust:** Tune in to your inner wisdom, allowing you to trust yourself and move forward with confidence.
- **Visualization:** Bring your desire to life by using all of your senses to experience it in consciousness.
- **Affirmation:** Use the power of your words to shift consciousness.
- **Self-love:** Empower yourself with self-love.

Remember to visit the book portal, which gives you access to recordings, worksheets, and additional information that can support you in implementing these pillars in your life.

Or go to:
https://www.joancoletto.com/heart-shift-book-portal

Perhaps you identified with one or more of the client stories I shared. Maybe it was Marin, who struggled to believe her dream of becoming a chef at her own restaurant was possible. Through the use of affirmations, visioning, and having a solid financial plan, she came to believe it was possible and is well on her way to realizing that dream.

Perhaps you related to Gary, who was always the victim, consumed by self-doubt with a wall built up around his heart. Through affirmations, visualization, and meditation, he transformed his relationship with his significant other and his work.

Or maybe it was Wendy, who had a vision of writing and illustrating children's stories that could make a difference in their lives. The clarity of her vision pulled her toward it and empowered her to leave her uninspiring job and take a chance on what she really wanted to do.

Embracing change with hope can lead to transformative experiences. My own journey into spiritual exploration began during a time of profound pain as I sought solace and guidance amidst the heartache of infertility and pregnancy loss. It was a search for healing, but what I found was a remarkable transformation in both my life and work.

Through my training in spirituality, hypnotherapy, and other modalities, I discovered not just a path to overcome my own struggles but also a profound source of joy in supporting others, second only to the love of and for my family. Witnessing the growth and change in individuals who once felt hopeless, as they become empowered to reshape their lives into freedom and joy, is an experience of joyous satisfaction that words can barely capture.

I share this to remind you that you, too, can reshape your life into what you deeply desire. The journey may start from a challenging place, but it can lead you to a life filled with joy, freedom, and fulfillment. Remember, where there is life, there is always hope for change and growth. You, too, can embrace this journey and live the life you've always desired.

Many blessings to you on your journey.

Resources

1. US Bureau of Labor Statistics. Monthly Labor review, June 2021, retrieved July 2023 from https://www.bls.gov/opub/mlr/2021/article/unemployment-rises-in-2020-as-the-country-battles-the-covid-19-pandemic.htm
2. Fair Health Inc. A Study of the Impact of COVID-19 on Pediatric Mental Health, March 2, 2021, retrieved July 2023 from https://s3.amazonaws.com/media2.fairhealth.org/whitepaper/asset/The%20Impact%20of%20COVID-19%20on%20Pediatric%20Mental%20Health%20-%20A%20Study%20of%20Private%20Healthcare%20Claims%20-%20A%20FAIR%20Health%20White%20Paper.pdf
3. World Health Organization. The impact of COVID-19 on mental health cannot be made light of, June 16, 2022, retrieved July 2023 from https://www.who.int/news-room/feature-stories/detail/the-impact-of-covid-19-on-mental-health-cannot-be-made-light-of#:~:text=A%20great%20number%20of%20people,anxiety%20or%20post%2Dtraumatic%20stress
4. Community Profile Book. Taber, Alberta, 2016, retrieved August 2023 from http://s3.arpaonline.ca.s3.amazonaws.com/Community+Profile+Books/Taber+CPB+2016.pdf
5. Dr. David Hamilton. The science of affirmations, January 27, 2022, retrieved August 2023 from https://drdavidhamilton.com/the-science-of-affirmations/#:~:text=University%20of%20Pennsylvania%20researchers%20showed,positive%20changes%20in%20people's%20behaviour.

Acknowledgments

This book was made possible through the love and support of many. It all began when Marsha invited me to a conference. I didn't know why I was there but soon found out that my long-ago desire to write a book had returned. Of course, it took a great deal of additional support, starting with Sara, Thought Leader Academy, and my editor, Hannah. Their unwavering support and wisdom were pivotal in the writing of this book. The writing days with Mark and Noelle were invaluable, and topping them off with a home-cooked meal and more love and support from Patrick was the icing on the cake. Thank you to Turbo for your gentle and consistent pushing beyond my comfort zone—it was sorely needed! A big thanks to Linda for designing a cover I love! Lastly, and certainly not least, to my mom, who has always been there for me, and to Mike, Lauren, Eric, Abbey, Ivy and Kylie—your support, as always, means the world to me.

About the Author

Joan Coletto is a hypnotherapist, spiritual practitioner, wife, mother, and grandmother. As the founder of Heart Shift her deepest desire is to make a significant difference in the lives of others, guiding them towards a path of healing and self-discovery. She works with people individually and through her membership community Transformational Living Community TLC.